HOW TO ANALYZE PEOPLE

Analyze and Influence Anyone - A
Psychologist's Guide to Speeding Reading
People and Personality Types

ERIC SKINNER

Introduction

Congratulations on downloading *"Analyze and Influence Anyone – A Psychologist's Guide to Speed-Reading People and Personality Types,"* and thank you for doing so.

We often want to understand the people we are dealing with entirely in terms of their thoughts, feelings, emotions, and motives. However, many of us do not know the first thing about analyzing people. Luckily, this book contains secrets to analyzing people - from the words they speak to the posture they take - everything that could get you to understand the other person better.

Your ability to read other people largely depends on how you deal with them. You will understand what the other person is feeling. You will have a clue about what is going on in his or her mind. You can predict their next course of action. With this information, you adopt an appropriate method of communication, message, or your behavior to enhance the interaction between you two.

To that end, the following chapters will teach you how to analyze people, and yourself too, to understand the drive and motive behind particular behavior and thought patterns. You will learn how critical the body language is in revealing the thoughts, attitude, and interest of a person. You will also learn how to monitor your behavior to see what hidden message your behavior could be suggesting. You will even get to know the cues to watch out for to know a person's true intentions besides learning about various tools you can take up to analyze behavior.

From reading this book, you will learn how to spot a lie, the benefits of asking questions instead of making assumptions, and how to find meaning in the words a person says. Besides, you will discover how to know that someone has the hots for you, or that you have developed a romantic interest in the person. You will learn how to identify insecurities in people so that you avoid getting drawn into their negative space (and possibly help them out of it).

There are plenty of books on this subject on the market, thanks again for choosing this one! Every effort was made to ensure it is full of as much useful information as possible. Please enjoy!

Watch the Body Language Cues

B ody language refers to the nonverbal cues used for sending and receiving information from one person to the other. Experts say that a great deal of our communication is done nonverbally through the body, even more than the words we speak. The communication is done through cues ranging from facial expressions to the movement of specific parts.

You communicate a volume of information even without saying anything. Research indicates that body language covers about 50 to 70 percent of all communication. This goes to show why understanding it is important; you could be missing much more information relying on words alone. However, it is best to interpret body movements as a group rather than each on its own.

Here are the things you should focus on when trying to read the body language:

The Eyes

Look out for the eyes. Many people say that the eyes are the windows to the soul; we have a bunch of love songs to claiming this. It is said that looking into a person's eyes can tell you so much about what the person is feeling or thinking. That is the reason we talk about seeing pain, love and a bunch of other emotions, through the eyes. Some people even say that they can tell when a person is lying from the eyes. Therefore, the next time you are conversing with someone, take notice of their eye movements. See whether the person maintains eye contact, or whether he averts his gaze. Check to see if the pupils are dilated, and how frequently the person is blinking.

Here's what to know about the eye signals mentioned above:

Blinking

Although blinking is natural, you should observe to see whether the individual is blinking too few or too many times. Rapid blinking is a sign of distress or discomfort. Infrequent blinking could be a sign that the person is trying to control his or her eye movements. A person playing poker will try to blink less frequently because he does not want to reveal the emotions he has in regard to the cards he is holding, whether excitement or disappointment.

Eye Gaze

When communicating with a person and the individual stares directly into your eyes, it means that the individual has an interest and is paying attention to what you are saying. A prolonged gaze is somewhat threatening while constantly breaking eye contact and looking away indicates that the individual is uncomfortable, distracted, and is trying to hide his or her true feelings.

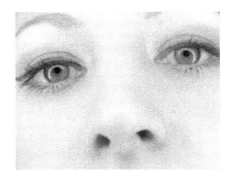

Some people believe that you holding on to someone's gaze is tough when you are lying to them. It is the reason most parents would insist that you look at them in the eyes when talking to them, and to an extent, they were right. However, everyone knows this now, and a person will deliberately maintain eye contact when lying as a cover-up. However, a majority of them overcompensate and tend to hold on to the gaze for longer, to the point that it feels uncomfortable.

. . .

On average, a person will hold a gaze for 7 to 10 seconds, but longer when listening in comparison to when the person is talking. If you hold a conversation with someone and his stare makes you uncomfortable, especially if the person is staring and not blinking, it is likely that something is up, and the person may be lying to you.

Size of the pupil

The size of the pupil is one of the most subtle communication aides. Typically, the pupil size is determined by the amount of light getting into the eye. However, emotions too cause variations in the size of the pupil. For example, you must have had the term "bedroom eyes." It is used to refer to the look someone gives someone to whom they are attracted. For this look, the pupils are dilated, and the eyelids sag a bit. This is also the look a person gives when he or she is aroused, sexually.

Hand Gestures

Hand gestures are some of the most obvious body language signals. They include pointing, waving, or using your fingers to signal numeral amounts. Some gestures have a cultural origin. However, some of the most common and popular hand gestures include:

- A thumbs-up or a thumbs-down: these gestures indicate approval and disapproval, respectively
- A clenched fist is a sign of solidarity, and in some situations, could mean anger
- The V gesture: this is the sign you create by lifting the index and the middle finger. The V shape created indicates victory or peace in some countries. However, in the UK and Australia, this symbol turns offensive, especially if you do it with the back of your hand facing outward.
- The okay or the all right sign: This gesture is made by making the thumb and the index finger touch while extending the other three fingers. It is used to indicate that things are fine. However, in some South American cultures, this is a vulgar gesture. In some parts of Europe too, this sign is used to indicate to a person that he or she is nothing.

The Mouth

Expressions done using the mouth are instrumental in conversations. They are also easy to note because you would be looking at the other party as they are talking or listening to what you say. For example, if a person is chewing on his or her lower lip, it could be that the person is feeling insecure, fear, or worry.

A person who is yawning or coughing will cover his mouth. However, this same act can be done as a way to cover up a disapproving frown. Smiling is possibly one of the most used body signals, but a smile could have a number of meanings too. A smile can be a way of expressing sarcasm, cynicism, or a way to fake happiness.

Lip biting indicates worry, stress, and anxiety. Having pursed lips by tightening them indicates disapproval, distaste, and distrust. Lips can also be turned upwards or downwards to suggest how a person is feeling. If the lips are turned slightly up, it could be that the person is optimistic and feeling happy. A slightly turned down mouth indicates the opposite- disapproval, sadness or a grimace. A relaxed mouth, on the other hand, suggests a positive mood and attitude.

. . .

A smile is either genuine or fake. A genuine smile is that which engages the entire face, but a phony smile only involves the mouth. A genuine smile is an indication that a person is genuinely happy and enjoying the company of those around him or her. A fake smile is intended to convey approval or pleasure, but in truth, the individual has a different opinion.

A half-smile is a smile that engages half the mouth, as its name suggests. The half-smile indicates uncertainty or sarcasm. You are also likely to notice a slight grimace for a second or two before a person smiles. This grimace should tell you that the person is masking his disappointment and dissatisfaction behind the fake smile.

A person who speaks while touching his lips or covering the mouth is likely to be lying.

Space

Most people do not consider space as body language. However, have you ever been in a situation where you felt uncomfortable because someone was standing awfully close? The distance between people who are interacting is called proxemics. Proxemics communicates a whole load of information, just like facial expressions and body movement.

There are four levels of social distance. The first is the intimate distance, which ranges from about 6 to 18 inches. This level of distance is indicative of a greater comfort or a closer relationship between two parties. This level of distance is apparent when people are engaging in intimate contact such as toughing, hugging and whispering.

The second level is the personal distance. It ranges from between 1.5 to 4 feet. This level of physical distance is common among close friends and family members. The closer the people are to each other, the more intimate their relationship.

The third level of distance is the social distance. It ranges from about 4 feet to 12 feet. Acquaintances keep this distance. The acquaintance could be someone you meet regularly, such as a co-worker, but one that you barely know. The relationship you have with the postal delivery guy also falls into this category.

The last one is the public distance. It ranges from between 12 and 25 feet. It is the kind that is used during public speaking, such as when talking to a class of students or giving a presentation at work.

The amount of personal space or distance that individuals need to be comfortable, however, is different between cultures. One example used often is the difference between the people of North America and those from Latin cultures. People from Latin countries feel comfortable standing close to each other in their interactions while those from North America insist on some personal distance.

Posture

The manner in which a person holds his body is also a critical part of their communication. The posture of a person is also defined as the physical form of the said individual. The posture offers a wealth of information about what a person is thinking and how he feels. It also hints at the individual's traits such as whether a person is friendly, confident, submissive or open.

For example, when a person is sitting straight, he indicates that he is paying attention and is focused on what is going on. Sitting with the body hunched forward suggests that the person is either indifferent or bored.

An open posture, by which the trunk of the body remains exposed and open indicates openness, friendliness, and willingness. This is often the way people will stay when they welcome you into their homes. A closed posture, on the other hand, involves hunching forward, hiding the trunk, and crossing the hands and the legs. This posture implies anxiety, hostility, and unfriendliness.

The Arms and the Legs

Your limbs also play a critical part in communication. Crossing your arms, for example, indicates defensiveness and an attempt to self-protect. Crossing your legs away from the person implies discomfort and dislike for them or the conversation. Crossed legs could also mean that the person is closed off, or is looking to have some privacy.

Widely extending your arms could be an attempt to appear larger and authoritative, but keeping your arms close to your body is often an effort to reduce the attention of others on yourself. Standing with your hands placed on hips indicates that the person is in control and ready. It is also a sign of aggression.

Clasping your hands behind your back shows that you are anxious, angry or bored. Tapping your fingers or fidgeting is a sign that you are frustrated, impatient and annoyed.

Unconscious pointing using the hands also speaks volumes. A person will occasionally point to the person he or she shares an affinity with.

Supporting the head with a hand that is resting on the table indicates that the person is paying attention and is holding his head to enhance his focus. Supporting the head with the elbows are resting on the table indicate boredom.

When a person holds out an object, placing it between him and the individual he is interacting with, the item serves as a barrier that blocks him from the other person. For example, if you are talking to someone and he goes ahead, picks up a pad of paper and places it in front of his face, the individual is trying to block or stop communicating with you.

The Movement of the Head

The speed of nodding the head as you speak will indicate to you whether your listener is patient, or not. Slowly nodding shows that the person is interested in what you have to say and does not mind moving along in the conversation. Nodding quickly is a sign of impatience: the person has had enough and desires that you finish speaking sooner, or that you should allow him to talk too.

Tilting the head sideways is a sign of interest in the conversation. Leaning it backward is a sign of uncertainty and suspicion.

. . .

People also tend to tilt their faces or their heads in the direction of people they like or share an affinity with.

If you attend gatherings and group meetings, you can easily tell the people with power in the group reading from how often people look at them. People who are less significant are looked at less often.

Mirroring

Mirroring is merely mimicking the body language the other person exhibits. When you are interacting with someone, check to see whether the person will mirror your behavior, your posture, and other aspects. For example, when sitting with someone at a table, place your elbow on the table, and wait about 10 seconds to see if the other person will copy you. Another mirroring gesture is taking a sip from your drinks at the same time.

When someone is mimicking your body language, it shows that the person is seeking to build a rapport with you. If you change your body posture, the other person should be changing his too.

The Direction of the Feet

When a person is sitting or standing, the direction to which the feet point is the direction the person wants to take. This could tell you whether the person considers you favorably or not. This cue is relevant both when having a one-on-one conversation and when talking in a group. In a group setup, the direction to which the people are pointed will tell you a lot about the group dynamics.

If you are having a conversation with someone, but his or her feet are pointing in someone else's direction, this is an indication that the person would instead be talking to the person to whom his feet are pointed towards, regardless of the cues you get from the upper body.

Other Body Language Indicators

Raised eyebrows

A person will raise his eyebrows to express worry, fear, and surprise. It would be impossible for you to raise your eyebrows when having an interesting, relaxed, casual conversation with a friend. If the person you are speaking to raises his eyebrows, but the topic you two are having does not contain any element of surprise, fear or worry, then something is definitely wrong.

Clenching the jaw

A tightened neck, a furrowed brow, and a clenched jaw are signs of stress. Regardless of the conversation going on, these signs indicate a high level of discomfort. You could be talking about something that the individual is anxious about or that the individual is focusing on something else that causes them to be stressed. The key is in identifying the mismatch between the conversation you are having and the boy language a person displays.

A pointed index finger with the rest of the hand closed

Figuratively, the pointed finger and clenched fist act as a club, and when a speaker uses it on an audience, he is beating them into submission. Most primates use this primal move before launching a physical attack. In response, this gesture evokes negative feelings in the audience.

A shaky leg

Legs occupy the most significant share of the body, and it is impossible not to see when they move. A shaky leg indicates irritation, anger, and anxiety.

A slight smile after making direct eye contact

A person who intends to seduce will give a specific kind of smile in a bid to look attractive, pleasant and seductive. The intention behind these gestures is to produce a positive effect. Sometimes, the seductive smile is accompanied by dominant behavior like glancing away slowly and with pride, or submissiveness like tilting the head downwards.

If the corners of the eyebrows do not move upward and inward

Psychologists refer to the muscles that you cannot contract voluntarily as reliable muscles. They say that if a person is expressing his sadness and frustration, likely to be using both words and facial expressions, but the corners of the eyebrows are not going in and up, then the person is possibly insincere. However much he tries, he will not be able to contract these muscles.

. . .

Expansive features

Ever noticed how leaders raise their hands in a V position especially during campaigns when they want to convince you that they are suited for the jobs they are vying for? Have you also noticed how athletes raise their hands too especially after winning a fight, a race or any other competition? They do this to indicate that they are powerful and that they have overcome in the competition. The individual gets into an erect posture, and walks down purposefully, making hand gestures and trying to get into an expansive body posture.

Expressing a bunch of gestures at a time

People do not show that they are attracted to others through one signal alone; they do it in a sequence of them. For example, if you look at the behavior of a girl who is attracted to you, or you look at a movie, once the couple makes eye contact, the girl blushes and looks down a little, then preens or gathers her hair, before looking back up at the guy with her chin tipped up.

If a person is laughing with you

A person who is receptive to your humor is plausibly interested in you. Researchers say that a positive reception to humor is a prerequisite and a signal for the desire of a relationship, whether romantic or platonic.

2

Take Note of Your Own Behavior

T he only things you have power over in your life are the things that come from the inside of you. They include thoughts, behavior, and feelings. Once you can manage them effectively, you will quickly achieve any goals that you may have for your life.

For you to gain this level of control, you must be aware of the scientific patterns behind your thoughts and emotions and know how to control or direct them. Once you are aware of how your mind works, you can intentionally influence the patterns in your life. You can also be better at evaluating the realities of your life, make better decisions, and enhance your capacity for achieving the goals you have set out. By doing this, you can conclusively determine, control and improve the quality of your life.

The Thinking Systems

So, how does the mind work? From a general view, you have two systems of thinking: the autopilot and the intentional system. The autopilot is run mainly by your intuitions and emotions. It depends on the cognitive processes that happen in the amygdala, those which helps us make quick decisions and reflexes, especially in life-and-death circumstances. This is also the system that determines your daily automated habits.

Since there are not many life-and-death stressors lying around, the autopilot system treats even the small stressors as such. This causes an unnecessarily stressful daily life experience that undermines a person's health and physical well-being. In addition, although the quick judgments we make based on emotions and feelings could feel right, they often lead people to the wrong predictable, systematic ways.

The intentional system is driven by rational thinking, and its processes are conducted in the prefrontal cortex. This thinking system gives you the ability to handle complex mental activities like handling group and individual relationships, probabilistic thinking, reasoning logically and learning new behavioral patterns.

While the automatic system does not require any conscious effort, the intentional system requires your effort to function. However, with the training that occurs as a person grows up, and the motivation to gravitate towards the right systems of behavior courtesy of the positive payoffs, the intentional system is ideal for situations when the autopilot fails or is likely to lead to mistakes. In most of life's circumstances, you will find that you need the intentional system better than autopilot because your system will rarely want to do the right things. You will not want to work too hard, to wake up early, to save your income, or do any other similar thing. Your body continually seeks comfort, but comfort discourages growth.

Recognizing Your Patterns

As you run on both autopilot and intentional systems, you are likely to develop patterns of behavior. Understanding yourself will require you to follow these behavior patterns so that you know when and how to intervene in them.

Although the concept of recognizing patterns is as simple as we say the phrase, the intricates of it is a little bit more complicated than that. One of the earliest patterns a human being takes knowledge of the language structure. Did you know that you can read a jumbled up word so long as its first and last letters stay in their place? This is only possible because you have learned to recognize the structure of the word.

When you looked at a misspelled word, what comes to mind is what you are used to seeing. If you saw the word "oredr" typed, the majority of us would read it as "order" because the brain will correct it to the version that you are used to seeing.

The same phenomenon is applicable in a whole load of things and events in our lives. The sequence of learning and adopting behavior in your life happens in these same stages. First, you establish the meaning of a particular occurrence. Second, you determine how different contexts can change the meaning of the event. Third, you determine what a repeat of the incident could elicit from you in terms of the action you should take. This entire process is what leads to the development of behavior: an event happens, you determine what it would mean in different contexts, and then you figure out what you will do about it. This process happens both when you are on autopilot and intentional systems.

Discovering Your Pattern of Behavior

Whenever you visit a therapist, the therapist asks you particular questions, and these questions are intended to discover various patterns in your life, of whom you might not be in knowledge. For example, you may go in there seeking help for your anxiety and stress issues, but the anxiety is only a symptom, and you need to get to the root of it to solve it. This is the reason patterns are of great help; following one will take you straight to the source of the problem.

Let's say you have developed the behavior of biting your nails all the time. Although you do not like it, you feel compelled to do it. Here are a few questions that you should answer to determine where your habit originated by establishing a pattern.

- What makes you feel like you should bite your nails? (it could be out of hunger, boredom, or the constant nudge telling you that they are uneven, so you want to even them out.)
- Where are you often when the urge comes up? (It could be that you do it anywhere, so long as no one sees you, but you are not shy around people).
- At what time does the urge to bite nails come mostly? (let's say it comes early in the morning and late in the evening.)

- Who, in particular, do you think causes you to bite your nails? (let's assume you will say "nobody").

In situations that are more specific, you have to ask the million-dollar question, why, for each of the answers provided. Look for relationships between the different factors, especially those that are not similar. For example, there are three distinct answers to the first question. The three options are not similar in any way, yet they result in the same behavior. You will want to ask yourself how hunger even pairs with the other situations listed. Ask yourself whether getting bored can trigger obsessive-compulsive behavior. For this case though, we have already established that the nail-biting was not born out of anxiety, and no person triggers it either. This does not form a pattern.

The fact that could somehow ease your understanding of the issue, in this case, is the timing. You have already established that you bite your nails, usually, in the mornings and in the evenings, which are typically the times of the day when you could be hungriest. You can now begin to explore in this direction. It could be that your diet is lacking in some nutrients, or that you are barely full, and that is why you get too hungry that you have to chew your nails. From then, you can substitute nail-biting with a snack or some food, and see whether you note any changes.

As you can see, the questions you ask provide a starting point that will eventually lead you to the root cause, so that you can understand behavior and its origins, with the option of making adjustments, to cause behavior change.

Understanding The Negative Behavior Patterns

It is easy to become hooked up to a behavior pattern that provides a psychological payoff, or a payoff of any other kind, even though it has some downsides. Examples of behavior like this include procrastinating, overeating, excessive spending and too much TV or internet. The way to overcome behavior like these is to understand the psychological payoffs associated with each. Once you know this, you will be more effective in handling the situation by establishing the psychological needs entangled in there and finding an alternative way of meeting these needs.

Some of the payoffs you are likely to seek in different habits and behavior include:

Emotional payoffs

An unwanted behavior comes with both positive and negative emotional payoffs. While you may be sad that you overslept, you get the thrill of making it in time for work or class. Most negative behaviors are associated with temporary feelings of reduced anxiety.

Physical payoffs

Physical payoffs are the intense, short-lived tangible benefits that keep you longing for the unwanted behavior. An example of a physical payoff is the energy rush that you feel after eating a snack with high sugar content.

Situation payoffs

Situation payoffs are the results you get out of doing something unwanted. For example, yelling at your child or your partner could get them to do what you want them to do. This is not to say that this behavior is right in the long-term.

Thought payoffs

The payoffs of having unwanted thoughts are a number. They distract you from thinking about a rather painful or troubling thing. They bring the illusion that the person is in charge of what happens to him or her; as a master of his or her destiny. The payoff changes how you think of yourself. Lastly, the payoffs cause you to believe that you deserve the excellent results you are getting.

Once you have identified the psychological needs entangled with the unwanted behavior, look for alternative ways to meet those needs. Be involved in the alternative methods at the time when you should be doing the unwanted behavior.

Your Personality Drives Your Behavior

The behaviors makeup that causes a person to be completely different from another is called a personality type. These behaviors are arranged into various categories, each comprising of two extremes, one on either side. Your behavior should fall somewhere between the two ends. Wherever your character is placed does not indicate superiority, not one of the labels on the scale is considered better than another. The groups include:

The Introvert/Extrovert

Within minutes of meeting a person, you can tell whether he or she is an extrovert or an introvert. Extroverts are good with networking, oral communication, and creating friendships with others. They are open and outgoing. However, they fail at listening, self-organization, following up on conversation and keeping appointments.

Introverts develop fewer stronger relationships and are better at written than verbal communication compared to extroverts. Introverts have trouble presenting themselves and their work, which often creates problems for them in situations where they have no choice such as in an office setup when they have to make presentations and sell their ideas. Some introverts are shy, although some are not, and they keep their emotions and thoughts to themselves.

Knowing to which category you will help you understand the benefits you can bring to the table, for yours and your team's advantage. It will also help you to understand some of the weaknesses you exhibit and possibly begin to work on them to reduce their influence. For example, if your nerves cannot allow you to speak in public, start some breathing exercises that could calm you down during an anxiety attack.

Whenever you want to make important decisions, you will want to see whether it is extrovert or the introvert in you that is leading you to a particular direction, or whether the decision is driven by rational thinking. Instead, you should speak yourself out of the comfort zone, and start to do what will steer you forward, into success.

Here are some of the questions you can ask yourself, depending on your personality type: As an extrovert, are you burning bridges by not giving relationships you have with people the weight and the respect they deserve? As an introvert, is the failure to speak up during important discussions keeping you from being recognized for your prowess in your field? Ask yourself either of these questions to determine the direction you want to take in life. Will you take action by learning how to speak better and address people, or will you cultivate the relationships around you better so you may have a constant source of support from them?

Your choice will determine how you behave, henceforth.

The Direct or Indirect

This dimension refers to the behavior a person displays towards others. Direct behavior is that which is concise and to the point.

Indirect behavior tends to include long conversations to avoid hurting anyone, maintaining political correctness. Extroverted people are liked for their direct approach, and some introverts also pick up on this trait especially when confronted and triggered to anger or defense mode by threats regarding their projects, families, and teams. The introverts speak up when they are cornered, and if the individual is task-oriented, he will not shy away from taking action.

Direct behavior often leads to tangible results because it inspires people to bring up opportunities and threats that could impact the team's performance. However, when overly done, the direct approach could easily spill over to rudeness and insensitivity. On the other hand, indirect behavior is passive, it helps maintain peace between individuals, but it slows productivity and progress. The long conversations could also lead to impatience and misunderstandings.

The Flight or Fight

The body's automated response to a bad situation is to either fight or run away. The fight or flight is not just for unexpected adverse events, it is also applicable to some bad situations that are not so dire, and they offer the individual an opportunity to make up his mind concerning the response he should give. Some people choose to fight while others take the flight option. A fight person will take a defensive and stubborn stance while a flight person will try to make an escape or to avoid the situation entirely. One factor that should matter, whether you take the fight or flight option is the effect that your behavior has on other people. If you take to flight, how is your lack of participation affecting your teammates? If you tend to fight back, you need to determine whether your fighting is challenging the safety of the people around you.

Change and No Change

Although some people are excited by change, others dread it. The way a person behaves will tell you whether he or she embraces change or doesn't. Many campaigners use change in their slogans as a vehicle for political success, but this does not mean that all people want to change. Change can bring significant positive results, such as start a revolution that changes the world, but it can also cause atrocities that lead people down an unattractive path. Resistance to change is a barrier to innovation, but it also helps to preserve time-tested strategies that have been a success all along.

Identifying where you lie in terms of change will help you re-evaluate your goals to see whether they are too rigid, or whether they focus on the right things. Check to see where your ideas will place you in the long-term especially in terms of making you more competitive in your field and in your ability to get the projected results.

Rebellious and Compliant

Each person has a unique view and an exceptional level of compliance with the rules and regulations that are in place. The attitude that a person has is purely based on his philosophical interpretation of life and within the person's behavior spectrum. A compliant person follows the rules strictly, whether or not they agree with the person's beliefs. He believes that he has a moral duty of obeying the laws.

A rebellious person bends the rules just of the sake of going against it entirely or, maybe, to achieve particular personal goals.

The behavior you portray in line with your following of rules will create either concern or excitement among them. Although being compliant is advantageous, a person should realize that some situations call for you to ditch the old rulebook and to pursue a different path. Besides, some rules do not make sense today, and their existence will prevent you from achieving success. Most countries in the world gained their independence by breaking the rules. Innovation and invention are also done by asking questions that go beyond the rules.

Fast or Slow

From the way an individual conducts his affairs, you can tell whether he or she is fast-paced or slow-paced. A fast-paced person holds his business at a terrific speed. He can think on his feet, and his speed makes him progress quickly and pursue new opportunities. However, this person can be reckless sometimes, and because of this, he could suffer irreparable damage.

A slow-paced person is one who carefully scrutinizes every step before he finally makes it. This person easily develops anxiety, especially in situations where resources like time are limited. Although behaving slowly will help you to avoid mistakes and pitfalls that other people fall to, it can also hinder opportunities.

The behavioral dimensions briefly discussed above are only a small number from a large lot. They represent some of the core influences of your behavior, and those of people around you. Taking note of these behavioral categories for yourself is impor-tant because when you know how to behave, you will be aware of how you communicate and act, and how that influences the rela-tionships you have. It is also important because while you can capitalize on the strengths, you have discovered, you can as well go ahead and work on reducing the influence and effects of your weaknesses.

3

Discover the True Intentions

Some people in this word are toxic, and you are better off recognizing their true nature before they unleash their true nature to you. Many of them appear friendly at first, but that is just a cover to fool you before they take advantage of you or manipulate into doing things that you would otherwise not do. To avoid being manipulated, there are some warning signs you can pick up to see through these people. Your intuition too will prove quite useful in this process.

The quick fix to the question of reading people is not to take things at face value. This is true because people are quite complicated, and you will need to think critically and to ask more questions regarding the people you meet.

Asking Questions

Many people do not care to ask some critical questions to the people they meet. Often, they fear that they will appear confrontational and rude. However, if you do it in a friendly way, getting the answers you need will enhance the relationship and the understanding between you and them.

For example, you could say, "Thank you for helping me carry my groceries to the car, but I wonder, why did you help me?" a question like this will open the window of communication and raises the sophistication of your conversation. Instead of it being formal, the conversation then changes to something personal, giving you both the opportunity to explore each's expectations and intentions.

By asking the question above, you will be seeking to know how the person relates to you, and to other people he encounters. You will see if the person expects something in return. You will also see how you relate to circumstances like these. The answers you get and how they are said will give you more to work with in regard to establishing the individual's true motives.

Rely on Other People's Judgment

I always say that you do not have to experience something for yourself to find out how bad or good it is; other people's opinions are critical, especially in keeping you from mistakes and pain. You should seek the advice of someone you trust, who knows the person you are dealing with. For example, if you are considering dating someone, go to someone who might already know the character of the potential date and could provide you with an accurate assessment of the person's traits.

If you are unsure of the intentions a person has towards you, go ahead and ask someone what they could read from the situation. For example, if someone keeps paying for your morning coffee, ask a friend or a colleague what that could mean. It is possible that the individual paying for your coffee is only a sociable and generous person and he does it from the goodness of his heart. It could also be that the person has developed an interest in you and is buying your coffee to catch your attention. Even more wildly, it is possible that the person buys coffee for any person he finds at the coffee shop, and you happen to be around at the time he comes. The list of possible reasons is endless.

Use Your Judgment

Your judgment is based on the information that you have accrued over time such that the new experiences you get can be compared to those of the past. In exercising judgment, the following questions can act as a guide:

For what reason, positive or negative, is this individual behaving as he is?

What reputation has the individual earned, through his interaction with me and with other people that I can use to relate to this latest event?

Drawing from the past, who else behaved in this same manner? What were the intentions behind that behavior?

Once you are able to remember of similar situations and think of the people that you have known in your life who could be party to the same, you will think from the point of judgment and information, and therefore make a wiser informed decision.

Keep Practicing to Make it a Habit

For everything you partake in life, so long as you increase the amount of work, dedication and time that you put into it, you will excel at. Analyzing people by correctly understanding their behavior and motives is one of those skills. It is considered a skill because when you verbalize what the other party is doing, which you are encouraged to do, this simple act causes neurons to fire up as they make connections throughout the brain. You might even literary feel this process going on inside your head.

You can practice reading motives in many ways just by going out, watching people and analyzing the motives the people have as they lead their normal lives. Think back to the moments in your own life that people acted out to you and you were unsure about their motives. Besides going out, you could also watch some people on YouTube and try to determine the reasons behind how they act or behave. Once you become quick and good at analyzing people's motives, it will be easier to do it in a short time in a different situation.

Analyzing people's motives will help you avoid getting manipulation through emotions. Some people thrive on emotion to lie and dupe people with their sad made up or exaggerated stories. Emotion is an excellent cover for the true intentions. However, when you can see through this manipulation, you will have greater control over the response you give, and the outcome of your interaction with the individual.

Rely on Your Intuition

It is possible to read into a person beyond the language he speaks and the words he says in a process called intuition. Intuition is your gut feeling, not the thoughts and ideas that you have. It is the unspoken information that you perceive from the images, the sudden realizations, and the knowing of the body rather than logic. If you really want to know what makes up a person, you ought to go beyond their physical makeup, and intuition allows you to do that.

Some of your intuitive cues include:

The feelings in your gut

Listening to your gut, especially when you meet a person for the first time will give you a close to an accurate determination of who a person is. It is an instinctual reaction that takes place before you engage your thought process. This reaction will tell you whether you are safe or not. It is your inbuilt truth meter that lets you know whether you can rely on people, or otherwise.

Flashes of insight

As the conversation is going, you are likely to experience flashes of insight. This is what people call the "ah ha" moments. In this case, the information about a person will come to you in a flash. You need to stay alert for this one; otherwise, you will miss it because thoughts will come bombarding you, such that you could easily lose your insights.

Notice the goosebumps

Goosebumps are the intuitive tingles that indicate that we connect to people who inspire and move us, in something similar to "striking a cord," or "experience a 'deja-vu,'" both of which indicate that you have known something or someone from a previous time in the past even when you have not.

Develop intuitive empathy

You can have some intense feelings about other people's emotions and physical symptoms in an intense form of empathy.

Tips to Help You Read Others

Establish a baseline

People display different patterns and quirks of behavior such as clearing their throat, crossing arms, stroking their neck, scratching the head, jiggling their feet, squinting, pouting, gazing at the floor when talking and many others. During an interaction, you may notice some and fail to notice others, and even those that you notice, you do not give much thought to.

What's interesting is that although we believe that people behave in a particular way to indicate the emotions and feelings they have on the inside, some could just be mannerisms that the individual adopted with time. For example, biting of nails is supposed to indicate nervousness and uncertainty, but this could be a bad habit a person has caught on.

Still, having a baseline for defining and understanding other people's behavior is still important because it will help you differentiate between what's normal and what's not.

Notice any behavior deviations

Take note of the inconsistencies between the baseline you have established, and the words or actions a person indicates. For example, you may have noticed that your doctor has a habit of repeatedly coughing to clear his throat whenever he is about to give you some bad news. Whenever he wants to talk to you about your increased weight, cholesterol level, and blood pressure, he begins by doing this. However, it could be that that's how he delivers all news, whether good or bad.

. . .

Therefore, you may want to study him or her further to know the different reactions he gives, so that you may know for sure that this reaction is a telling sign that not all is well.

Take note of the clusters of gestures

A single gesture is similar to a single word: it means nothing. However, when several gestures and words are brought together, you ought to take notice of that. Ensure that you derive meaning out of it. For example, if you walk into your doctor's office and he continuously clears his throat, looks at you with concerned eyes, leans with his back arched forward looking at you in the eye, you ought to be concerned and to pay attention because what is to come next may not be good.

Make a comparison

When you notice that someone is acting differently than you know them to act, keep observing to see if the person will behave differently when interacting with others. This is the first sign that you are losing touch with someone, especially if the person is mistreating you and being kind to others. For example, if your spouse is kind to others and is mean to you, realize that something has stained your relationship and dig deep to see what it could be.

Once you have resolved your issue with your friend or partner, observe again, how he or she interacts with the people around. See whether the person's expressions change, especially in regard to how the person treats you. How about his body language and posture?

. . .

Identify the source of influence

The individual that has the most power is not always the one seated at the head of the table. The most powerful of the people sitting around a conference room table is the most confident one. You will notice him by his strong voice, expansive posture, and possibly, a smile. Be careful, however, that you do not confuse a loud voice with a strong one.

If you are presenting an idea to a group, you may feel compelled to lay much of your attention to its leader. However, in some cases, the leader could have a weak personality and will rely on other people to make a decision. If you read into this as you study the dynamics of the group, focus more of your attention to the most influential voice in the group, and you are likely to achieve success in what you are pursuing.

Look for cues that could suggest to you the individual's personality

Individuals fall into four different kinds of personality classification, and there are characteristics common to each personality type. Identifying some of these characteristics will significantly help you read into the person accurately, even before you move further along in your conversation.

For example, check to see if the person is an introvert or an extrovert. See whether relationships drive the person or not. See how the individual handles uncertainty and risk. Look to see what seems to feed his ego. How does the person behave when he or she receives terrible news or is stressed? How does the person behave when happy and relaxed?

Take note of action words

The easiest way to get into a person's head is through their words. Words are drawn from a person's thoughts, and you should take note of the word that carries the most meaning. For example, if your friend tells you that she has chosen to marry a particular man, the action word there is "chosen." This word suggests that your friend has given the idea some considerable thought, she did not make the decision hurriedly, and that weighed several options before finally settling for the individual she is marrying.

Action words used will help you understand a person's thought process. The word chosen" has a different meaning to if the same friend told you that she had thought of marrying. If she used the word "think," you would probably follow it up with "Are you sure?" or "For how long have you thought about it?" think suggests that the decision was reached hurriedly, and it was not well thought out, which leaves room for mistakes.

Watch to see how the person walks

Sometimes, a person will shuffle along, without any rhythm or flowing motion to his movement. Other times, he walks with his head bowed due to lack of confidence. If you notice these signs in a person you are dealing with, make an effort to offer a compliment to the individual. A compliment works wonders in boosting the individual's confidence. If you are having a discussion with him, ask him some questions; most shy people have a lot of wisdom and insight to share, they only need to be asked questions so that they may open up.

In conclusion, reading into someone to determine who exactly the person is is very important. It goes beyond the words that the individual speaks, his body language, or body movement. If you depend on these alone, you would not be able to see the person past the mask he puts on. Although asking questions is an important strategy too, it is not sufficient by itself. In addition, compiling facts and logically analyzing them will not tell you the person's entire story either. You must involve critical inherent and intuitive clues, from you and the individual you are studying.

For this to be done effectively, however, you ought to surrender any preconceived ideas or the emotional baggage you may have got from your interaction with the said individual in the past. Any resentments or admiration you have could cloud your judgment and prevent you from seeing the individual clearly. The key to the remaining objective in this entire process is to avoid distorting the information you receive.

4

Cues to Point You to the True Intentions

When you newly know someone, knowing precisely what the person's intentions can be difficult. Is the person a fraud or is the business deal he is presenting legit? Does the person maintain a calm spirit or does he sometimes erupt with anger and wreak havoc to all who are around him? If the person is attracted to you, is he there for a one-time thing or is he looking for a committed relationship? Does the person have your interests at heart or are you just a means to him satisfying his needs? Many questions come up when you newly know someone. Sadly, the answers to them cannot be got from a few hours of conversation. These hours sometimes turn into days, months and even years without getting to know a person's true self.

Cues That Indicate Ill Intentions

Ultimately, since in most occasions, an individual will appear good to you, whether he meant well or not, you ought to know the cues that indicate bad intentions, at least, and if they do not come up, enjoy the positive side. Being aware of the bad will help you avoid the bad ones like the landmines they are. If the person turns up happy, then you are unmarried and looking for the individual with a calm spirit.

Here are some ways that can help determine a person's true intentions:

The person talks about what a nice person he is

While a person may make an effort to sell himself if he has come to you with a business idea or is attracted to you, it is unlike people to start talking about how virtuous they are. A person of virtues will not even want to tell you his good qualities; he waits for you to identify them yourself. Therefore, when a person comes to you claiming how good he is, he isn't. He is only trying to cover his real character.

In the same way, a person who insists that he is not a threat and makes requests that you should show him around your business, or your home, this isn't the kind of person you should trust or give your time to. That person could be interested in other things and not what he claims. He could be a thief.

Remind yourself that you have met a bunch of nice people in your life before, and none pestered you to know that they are good, you learned all by yourself. Every other person that comes into your life you will know in the same way.

.   .   .

The individual seeks to charm you instead of getting to the business of the day

When a person or a group of people is being insincere about their intentions towards you, they are likely to go a very long way to get you to pay attention to other issues besides what is important. For example, people who would want to defraud you, but have presented themselves as suppliers of a particular item will want you to discuss your check-in account more than the relationship they wish to establish with you. A lady who is not genuinely interested in a man will be shallow in her conversation, not wanting to know more about the man, and instead of showing interest in things like gifts, money and others, instead of getting to know the man genuinely.

An insincere person is all about surface appeal and will create an image so good that neither you nor others like you will doubt his sincerity. He or she will dress the part, and look like a big shot. He will tell you all the things that could traditionally impress you depending on the context of your relationship, without putting any effort to learn about what you do. This attitude leaves you vulnerable and open to his efforts, and this does not produce any good results.

For example, a fraudulent businessperson will talk about how he or she knows the secrets to get the government contract you have been looking for. He will even show you fake contact names of people in government that he calls for deals like those. You will be charmed by his success and not even consider the information gaps in his story. Charmed out of your socks, you will give in to him, and lose money in the process.

. . .

There are no people with whom you can reference the information you get

So far, the person you have met will seem like the dream. Everything he says may even have checked out so far. The company he claims to own may exist (but it is likely that he is not affiliated to it), but there is no one to confirm anything you have been told. You won't find a company or business he has worked with in the past. If you ask around, people do not even know that the business exists. If it is a man looking to have a relationship with you, he will not have any friends.

Toxic people and frauds rarely have friends most likely because the people who knew them got wind of the terrible character and walked off. People with bad intentions also do not see the need to keep people around especially those that will not offer them the benefits they desire. All that the person will care about is the gains he can get, and you are at the center of it all.

Only one thing in mind

The only thing that the person has on their mind is to get you to do his or her bidding. The only reason the person has you around is that you are a means to an intended end. If the person wants to have a hundred thousand dollars, you have the money in your account, and you are the only means to that money. Once he gets the money, then your association with him is as good as dead.

You will see that the person will form a pattern with his or her talking about the same things, in an attempt to convince you to do what they need you to. The person believes that if you hear that thing enough times, you will subtly slide into the same mind frame that he is in, and then get you to make the decision, as though both of you came to it, even if you were just trickled into making that decision.

Information about the person and his intentions are vague

A direct bad sign that the person you are dealing with is insincere is that he or she comes to you with vague information. If he is seeking a relationship, the man will say that he does not believe in labels, and so, there is no need to refer to each other by particular title so long as everything between you two is great. You will see sense in this argument, but at the back of your mind, there will remain a gnawing reminding you that you wanted a healthy relationship, not a directionless union.

There are also situations where a new friend will know evertyth9ng there is to know about you. He or she will come to your house, to your job place, will meet your family and other friends, but you will not have the same information about them. You will not have an idea where the individual lives, where he or she works, no idea about the friends, or any other personal information. In a situation like this, ask yourself one question: what is the reason behind this anonymity? What could this person be hiding?

The individual is too needy

It is never a good sign when a person becomes too needy and places all these demands on you, especially if you are new to each other. When a person has already started making demands in regard to your time and commitment to him, the alarms in your head should be blaring already. This is a clear sign that something much darker lies ahead.

For example, if a new boyfriend always demands to know where you are, what you are doing, the people you are with and the time when the person should expect you- or that he texts you all day to make sure that you are within reach, you are about to get into some weirdly manipulative territory. In addition, if all you do is cater to his needs for attention, time, money and others, realize that the entire relationship will be about him, from the start to the end.

Neediness in a relationship is not a cute sign to show that someone is obsessed with you and so in love that he cannot spend a minute without you. You will know this because the thought of being with that person will have you worrying rather than dreaming of champagne toasts and wedding dresses.

Trust the animals

Animals are great at sensing things. If you bring the person home and your cat or dog that is typically relaxed around people and creeps out, but now the animal is showing some level of hostility towards the new person, be alarmed, and take that as a sign. This is not to suggest that your pets should lead your decisions, it is only to say they have a special instinct and can pick up on things that we ignore as humans.

.   .   .

If the person does not care for the pets or is even cruel to them, take this also as a sign of how the person treats other people, especially those that are weaker or smaller than he is. A person's emotions do not vary when the individual is dealing with animals and people: you cannot be cruel to animals, but kind-hearted to people. Therefore, the treatment a person gives to your pets is a good indicator of the relationship that he or she has with others.

The person won't let things go

Holding a grudge is different from an unwillingness to let things go and sweating the small stuff. It is ugly when a person uses small issues as a point of contention time and gain. For example, if someone accidentally steps on the toes of your potential business partner and he cannot stop cursing and hurling insults at the person, this is a sure sign that the man is bad news. If small things like that cause him to be so erratic, how about when significant things happen? You would be at the receiving end of extreme bile.

This is also the measure to use when dealing with a potential romantic partner. If the partner shows uncontrollable anger because of small things, or even the big ones, you are only digging your grave by getting together with someone like that.

A person who flies so off the handle does not have any good intentions to you because he considers what you have done so bad because they are not sticking to the narrative he had planned out. When things change a bit, he feels that his control and power is being challenged.

. . .

A person who is not willing to let some things to slide is an ache to have around. No one wants to live with or work next to all that negativity.

The person mounts too much pressure on you

A person with bad intentions will pull out all the stops to manipulate you into doing his bidding. This person is a master manipulator and will do whatever it takes to ensure that the people around him work to achieve his ends. If you get into a relationship with a person like this, be prepared to stop living your own life, and instead, start living to please the person. He or she will pressure you to do things for him or her and will throw incredible tantrums if you don't do it.

The process of pressuring you to nudge you in the direction that the person wants you to go is like a game to him. Even if you refuse to do it countless times, the guy will continue to poke and prod at you, until you give in. Belittling and gaslighting are some of the most popular methods used. Some become emotional and will tell you a few emotional stories, made up or exaggerated so that you feel obligated to offer help and consolation. He or she takes advantage of the empathy you have, all the while not caring about the lengths you will go to meet his or her needs.

If you get into a relationship with a person like this, he or she will get mad, will not pick your calls, and will act withdrawn to throw you off your game. Since you do not want the drama and the emotional baggage, you will dance to the individual's tune. This way, the person will have control over you, and slowly, your life will be about pleasing that person, having forgotten about yourself.

Body language tells it all

The body language communicates the intentions a person has. If it seems off, then it probably is, and you ought to get as far as possible from this individual. If you notice the limbs making some irregular jerking movements, sweating, an inability to be comfortable, averting his eye from yours and covering the mouth and nose when speaking, you should know that something about this person is off, and shouldn't trust him.

A person with bad intentions is fully aware of his behavior and has a rough idea of how you would react if you got to know about his act. In most cases, they feign normalcy and will try to act as though they are not convincing you to get in on whatever they are doing, and where they intend to lead you.

Therefore, pay attention to the way a person speaks and behaves in a normal conversation when speaking to you or another person, and compare this to how he speaks to you when talking about the relationship, the business deal, or any other issue that got you communicating.

Notice the neg

A person who has no good intentions for you will neg to get your attention. Negging is an old trick of the book where a person will insult you cleverly in a way that gets your attention, gets you defensive, and in the process, makes you attracted to the person. The individual tries to play the insult as a joke, even though he does not get anyone to laugh. This is a terrible way of getting someone's attention, and a person who takes up this habit does not know a thing about decency.

A person who has good intentions towards you would never insult you, whether as a joke or otherwise. He will respect the relationship he is trying to create (romantic, business or any other kind), and treat you with respect for the sake of the future. He will, therefore, observe all the words that come from his mouth, and be concerned about the effect that they have on you. In addition, negging is proof of the poor view of you that the person has.

The person doesn't speak the truth

Telling a white lie here and another there is all right, especially if the lies are said to protect another person from something trivial that he would be better off not knowing. For example, telling your friend that you are running late because the traffic is terrible is better than having to tell the truth, that you couldn't miss an episode of your favorite daytime talk show like The Ellen Show.

That said, a person with bad intentions does not stop at the little white ones, the person goes full blast and lies big time, even when it is unnecessary to do so. Liars are known to generate toxic ideas and live toxic lives, so when you realize that the person lies a lot, remember that he or she is only looking to damp the toxicity on to you.

. . .

These liars lie to make themselves look nice, to get their way or to obtain trust, and all these tactics are laden with evil intentions.

The person is not willing to be seen with you

This point mostly applies to romantic relationships. When a person is dating someone, he or she admires and respects, there's an eagerness to show the person off to the entire world. In fact, the person will want to be seen walking next to you, with his hands clasped tightly to yours. However, if the man does not want to be out in public with you, and only wants to meet you in the dead of the night, you ought to know that the person is not invested in you and that the relationship you two have is primarily meant to meet his needs, and if possible, not mandatory, yours too.

While this is a character synonymous with men, ladies have picked up on the habit too, and are using men for their benefits, without considering the emotional state of the men they are with.

5

Behavior Analysis Tools

You have met someone for the first time just now. How long will it take you to size this person and come up with a first impression?

Many people will tell you that it would take them at least a minute to come up with something, but in reality, they do it faster than that. Scientists have found that it only takes a tenth of a second to develop a first impression of someone based solely on his body language. In fact, you do not need the person to talk to read into the individual's personality because psychologists say that only about 7% of our communication is done orally, the more significant proportion of the conversation is done using nonverbal messages and vocal cues.

If the majority of the communication is done using the physical body language, how will you know whether you are reading into the language correctly? You need reliable tools and techniques to help you analyze behavior a little easier, and with more accuracy.

Behavior Analysis Techniques

Below are techniques you can use to analyze the behavior of a person you meet or are in close contact with.

Read from the emotional energy

Emotions are an excellent expression of the energy or the vibe a person is giving, and you only register these emotions using your intuition. For example, it will feel good to be around some people because they bring an improvement to your vitality and mood while some people drain your emotional energy, so much that you will want to get away from them immediately. You will sense the emotional energy when you get to a few inches or feet from a person.

To read a person's energy, use the following strategies:

Watch the person's eyes

The eyes are powerful transmitters of energy. Science indicates that just as the brain transmits an electromagnetic signal that extends beyond the body, the eyes have a signal too. Therefore, whenever you interact or are about to interact with people, be careful to observe their eyes. Do you sense anger, aggression, peace, attraction or meanness? Does the person appear guarded and hiding?

Sense the person's presence

Our bodies emit overall energy that surpasses behavior and words. This energy is the emotional atmosphere that surrounds a person. As you read into the energy that the person is transmitting, see whether the presence is friendly. Does it attract you to the person or do you have an urge to back off?

Listen to the laugh and the tone of voice

The tone and the volume in a person's voice will tell you much about your emotions. As you read into a person's behavior, notice how his or her voice affects you. Does the tone sooth you, or is it snippy, abrasive and whiny?

Notice the touch, the hug, and the handshake

Physical contact acts as the wire that completes an electric circuit. Does the handshake or hug the person gives feel comfortable, warm and confident? Does it off-put you so much that you want to withdraw? Is the hand clammy to show anxiety or is it limp, which indicates timidity or a lack of commitment?

Behavior Analysis Tools

The following are scientific tools used to study and analyze behavior:

Observation

Observation is the process of attentively and carefully watching for, listening and studying the subject in his or her natural environment. Behavior analyzed using this method is studied either directly or indirectly. Direct observation is the process in which the practitioner himself watches the subject while indirect observation is the analysis of behavior that is dependent on the report of others who have been observing the study subject.

You conduct direct observation analysis of behavior to look for data that could develop and support the hypothesis you have regarding particular behavior and its triggers. You must observe when the behavior in question occurs, what triggers the behavior, the antecedent behavior, how the behavior you are studying plays out, and how other people around the subject respond to the behavior, the consequences.

Direct observation

Direct observation is the basis for conducting various behavior assessments and evaluations. By observing the subject directly, the observer gets to learn about the behavioral traits, weaknesses, strengths, and special characteristics that a person might have. Anyone who is exposed to the subject will observe behavior using this direct method. However, you must conduct this observation in a way that the subject will not know that he or she is being observed. The presence of an observer could lead to a change in behavior in what is called the Hawthorne Effect (nnnn).

Functional direct observation takes place when an observer gathers enough data that can answer the question asked, such as to understand why a person behaves the way he does, the stimuli that trigger particular behavior, and the action that can be taken to cause a change in behavior.

. . .

For example, if you notice a child mimicking the body movement of a person living with a disability, such as a limp, you already have established the environmental factors that should change to reduce or cut down the child's behavior. For example, counsel could greatly help by helping the child to understand the reason behind the limp, and the reasons the child should not start limping unnecessarily.

Play-based direct observation

This method of observation is done in circumstances that involve the formal and informal behavior of the subject. The behavior the subject exhibits in regard to his or her communication, social and emotional behavior is observed. For example, you could stand at the counter at the store to see how the cashier interacts with the customers in his natural element. By observing how the employee treats the customers, one by one, you will be able to establish a pattern or style of interaction that the person uses.

Indirect observation methods

Indirect observation is a technique through which behavior that happened and was recorded in the past during an event, a conversation or any other encounter with the study subject. Since it is an account of what another person observed directly, the material used in these methods are transcriptions from audio recordings of some words that were said in a natural setting or directly from the words the interviewee will say. It may also include other additional items that would increase the relevance and more details of the events described.

. . .

All the material used makes for a rich source of information to study behavior exhibited daily. These information sources are also growing every day, courtesy of the technology advancements that are making recording, dissemination, and storage much easier.

Narratives are an excellent source of reliable second-hand information. However, the source of information should be viable and objective.

The ABC Chart

The Antecedent-Behavior-Consequence (ABC) chart is a tool used to assess and gather information about behavior that evolves into a positive behavior support plan. The antecedents are the behaviors a person exhibits before conducting the behavior. Behavior is how the subject of the study holds himself or herself. Consequences are the responses or the actions that follow after the behavior.

ABC (Antecedent, Behavior, Consequence) Chart Form

Date/Time	Activity	Antecedent	Behavior	Consequence
Date/Time when the behavior occurred	Which activity was going on when the behavior occurred	What happened right before the behavior that may have triggered the behavior	What the behavior looked like	What happened after the behavior, or as a result of the behavior

The ABC method is sometimes considered to be among the direct observation methods because the observer has to keep an eye on behavior as it occurs. This method is applicable only for when a person is free and can observe behavior. It is taken up when an observer is available at the specified times to make observations. The method is personnel and time sensitive,

While it is important to think about the antecedents and the form of behavior, the focus of many is on the consequence portion of the chart. Examine this portion when you want to identify the responses that increase or decrease. For example, if giving someone attention increases his problem behavior, then it is only wise to teach the individual to seek that attention in a better fashion or to use the attention just for positive behavior.

If escape from a difficult task is a typical reaction in the consequence section, then the appropriate course of action is to either change the task or to ask for help completing it. The response you give, however, should focus on increasing the chances of having the desired behavior, promoting replacement behavior and decreasing the frequency of occurrence for the problem behavior. One of the important things to do, however, is to understand the consequences or the responses and whether they will increase, decrease or maintain the current responses.

The Scatter Plot

The scatter plot a tool used to collect information about a

problem behavior at specified intervals throughout the day. The scatter plot useful for determining whether behavioral problems occur at the same time of the day, at predictable times, or not. The information collected using the scatter plot is useful for identifying the right intervention method, and to determine the routine of effecting the methods.

The scatter plot a grid with the time variable plotted on the vertical line and divided into various times. For example, the time interval between the markings could be 15 minutes, 30 minutes or 1 hour each, depending on the time it took to conduct the study. The horizontal line indicates the designated days during which the observations were made.

In a functional behavioral assessment, the scatter plot supports direct observation to identify the times when the specified behavior occurs. One advantage of this grid is that the number of measurements strategies can be used to indicate the frequency durations, frequency counts, and the latency recording. For example, another way to make the recordings is to use a particular symbol to indicate the low rates of occurrence, and a different symbol to indicate the high rates of occurrence. You could also indicate the exact number of times that the behavior was observed into the cells.

The disadvantage of this tool, however, is that it does not give the observer an opportunity to indicate the consequences and the antecedents that he notices, which means that the observer will need to indicate additional recording in his assessment.

Record Reviews

Record reviews are excellent for observing and analyzing the subject's behavioral and psychological reports recorded in the past, which provides critical information about an individual's social skills, possible setting events, academic problems or strengths, and issues that have to do with the quality of life. The old behavioral support plans will indicate to you the trend of problematic behavior, and the intervention offered, pointing to the methods that have succeeded in the past.

Looking at abandoned behavioral support plans will tell you of the types of intervention methods that failed, and could not be a good fit for the person to whom the method is to be implemented, or even for those that are implementing it. It is also possible for a person going over these reviews to come up with information that describes a setting where the study subject experienced success and did not take part in the problem behavior.

The kind of records to be reviewed using this method include psychological records, mental health information, individual education or family service plans, old behavior support plans, and allied health provided assessments, such as the results of occupational, speech and language therapy. Accessing this material requires special permission, and the observer needs to maintain confidentiality in regard to the number of people that can obtain this information.

The advantage of using record reviews is that this method is quick and easy to complete. Completing the assessment early will give the team adequate time to consider the variables that could be affecting behavior, especially those that may not be obvious.

A disadvantage of this method, however, is that the materials that are reviewed may not necessarily indicate the current state of the subject. The behavioral support plans of the past may be targeting a person's childhood behavior and using them to analyze behavior today may not reflect the person as he or she is today, whether a teen or an adult. In addition, this method is not as objective as other methods like direct observation. However, combining this method with others like direct observation will enable you to conduct one of the most useful assessments because you will be able to trace the trends and the origins of behavior, and you will have a clue about the intervention methods that have been used in the past, whether successfully or otherwise.

Interviews

Holding interviews with key people helps to determine various perspectives and concerns that others may have in regard to the study subject. For example, if you are unsure of the character and behavior of someone you had hoped to do business with or to marry, you could ask unbiased people who know the person whether he or she would be a suitable candidate for whatever you intend to do with them. Interviews also help to identify the events that are associated with the occurrence, or lack thereof, of the behavior of interest.

For example, if a teacher reports that a student has been engaging in unfavorable behavior in the classroom, the teacher should be called upon to participate in an interview so that he or she can offer more information regarding the same. However, the teachers who may have a different opinion because the student does not indicate the said behavior in their classrooms could be called upon to offer their insights too. The student too, the parent, his friends, and other people who may provide useful insight to the study are also called upon to provide answers to the questions asked.

In the end, the responses collected are used to determine the triggers of the said behavior based on the direct evaluations made by various parties in the subject's life. The information derived from this study is used to understand the reasons behind the behavior portrayed and to establish possible methods of intervention that could help the student behave better in school, during all the learning sessions. It also becomes the basis for eliminating various triggers of negative behavior.

6

The Meaning Is in the Words

Words indicate what is in the mind because words are drawn from thoughts. The closest you can get to understand a person's thoughts is by listening to him or her speak, or by reading the written content. Some words directly indicate the behavioral characteristics of the person from whom they originated. Some people call them word clues. Word clues make it easier to analyze behavioral traits, but they are not sufficient to get you a complete analysis because some insincere people are quite choosy with their words, and have a sweet tongue that will cause you to make favorable conclusions, while that is not the individual's character. This does not mean, however, that the word clues are inefficient, they are.

Function and Content Words Usage

The brain is an incredible and efficient organ, and gladly, we can study it. When a person thinks, he or she only uses nouns and verbs only. The rest of them, the adverbs, adjectives, articles, conjunctions, auxiliary verbs, prepositions, and others, are just added during the speech or in writing. These added words, besides the noun and the verb, are the ones that say something about your character, behavior, and personality. They also indicate the individual's stability, honesty, and sense of self.

This discovery was made in the 1990s when James Pennebaker was involved in the development of a computer program that categorized and counted words in texts, differentiating between function words and content words. (Function words are the pronouns, adjectives, conjunctions, prepositions, and others that we listed before). The study analyzed more than 400k texts, which included SMS from lovers, essays submitted by college students, press conference transcripts, and chat room discussions. Pennebaker found that function words were the key elements towards determining the psychological state of a person. They revealed much more information than the content words did.

A basic sentence contains a verb and a subject. For example, in the sentence, "I ate," "I" is the pronoun, which is also the subject, while "ate" is the verb. Any other words that you could add to this basic structure will change the quality of the verb and the noun. However, these additions will accurately let you in into understanding the clues to the behavioral and personality characteristics of the writer and the speaker.

Using the word clues, you can come up with hypotheses or make educated guesses regarding the other person's traits and behavior. For example, if you say, "I showered quickly," the word "quickly" introduces a sense of urgency, but the reason that necessitated the urgency is yet unknown. The quick shower could be because the person is late for something or anticipates lateness.

A person who is worried that he or she is late is one who respects the social norms and wants to live according to other people's expectations. People with behavioral characteristics like these make good friends, partners, parents, and employees because they do not like to disappoint others.

There are also many other things you can learn about the person. For example, because the person took a quick shower, it means that the person values personal hygiene and the comfort of those he or she will be around. It also suggests that the person does not want to miss the bus or run into traffic, and therefore, this person has established some form of structure in his life that he does not wish to mess up. If he gets to work by 6:00 am, then he must do all he can to arrive by then. The reasons for adding 'quickly' to his sentence are numerous, but there is only one drive to behavior.

Words are an effective noninvasive technique to help you read through the words a person speaks, even without their knowledge.

Let's look at another example. If a person says, "I wrote another song," the statement conveys the idea or the information that the individual has written one or many other songs in the past. He or she wants other people to realize that there is a new addition to their list of songs, possibly to bolster the person's self-image and to get others to issue compliments and admiration for the achievement, which will boost the individual's self-esteem. The people around this individual could choose to exploit this vulnerability by use of flattery and other comments to enhance the individual's ego.

Motivational speeches from people who seem to have achieved success in life (success is relative), often contain the statement, "I worked very hard to achieve the success I now have." You could also have used this statement sometime. Let's break it down. The first-word clue is "hard" and it suggests that the person values the success he had in achieving the goal he attempted to reach. It could also mean that this specific goal that the individual has achieved is more challenging to accomplish than others that the individual attempts to achieve.

The word "hard" also indicates that the person can defer gratification, or holds that to get good results, a person must be hard-working and dedicated to what he is doing. An applicant to a job who has this mindset would make a good employee because he or she will be accepting of the challenges he or she meets, and will retain the determination to complete the task successfully.

Interestingly, if you ask somebody a question and the individual replies with an "I," that the person is somewhat self-obsessed. For example, if you ask, "How is the weather today?" and the person gives you an "I think it is rainy," and not "It's rainy," the "I" should tell you much about that person. Depressed people tend to use "I" much more than emotionally stable people. People who consider themselves to be of a lower status than others do the same too.

When a person is lying, he tends to use "we" more, or use sentences that do not have a pronoun at all. For example, instead of saying, "I did not steal your wallet," the liar will say, "A person with integrity shouldn't be caught stealing." An honest person tends to use particular words like "without," "but," "none," and "never" more frequently. Courts take note of the use of this kind of words to determine whether the testimony is true or not.

The use of function words varies across genders. Most people would assume that men use "I" more because they are considered self-congratulatory and narcissistic. However, studies show that women use first-person pronouns more often because they are self-attentive. This means that they are more aware of their inner state in comparison to the men.

Men, on the other hand, tend to use "a," "an," and "the," which indicates that men have a tendency of referring to concrete objects more because articles often precede the use of nouns. Women also tend to use third-person pronouns like "he," "she," and "they" because they tend to speak more about other people and relationships because they are better at keeping an account and managing them.

You can also detect that a person is a suicide or depression risk by his use of function words. Writers and public figures use singular first-person pronouns when they feel suicidal or depressed, which is an indication of possible social isolation and self-absorption.

Age is also a factor in the use of function words. A person refers to himself less as he ages. He also tends to use more words that convey positive emotion rather than negative ones. He also takes up the use of more future-tense verbs and fewer past-tense verbs.

Words Reflect Character

The words you speak reflect your character. This is especially true with regard to how a person speaks about another. Specifically, when a person speaks negatively about another, it not only hurts the person they are talking about, it also negatively reflects on the speaker's reputation and credibility. Richard Carlson said that whenever you speak ill of another person through criticism and judgment, the words you speak do not say anything about that person. Instead, they reflect on your need to be critical. Therefore, whenever you talk negatively about another person, realize that others will see it as a ploy to make yourself feel and look good at the expense of another, even when what you are saying is true.

You must also realize that wherever your reputation goes, there will your emotional energy be. If you focus on positive things such that your speech becomes positive too, your life will be positive. However, if you focus on negative things, everything in your life will become negative also. Whenever you speak negative words about someone, the negative energy you generate in the process will also affect your life. It is impossible to speak negative things about someone and remain happy yourself. Your mood tends to dampen too.

A person who brands himself as one who will not speak negatively or disapprovingly of others makes them respect him, and in the end, he leads a happier life. When you keep yourself from speaking negative things about other people, especially when the opportunity to trash them arises, you increase your self-control and your concern for other people. Dale Carnegie says that any fool can condemn, criticize and complain, but it takes self-control and character for a person to be forgiving and understanding.

Kindly also note that there is a difference between speaking in a derogatory way and criticizing someone formally such as talking to the individual about his performance review, or when pointing out someone's deficiencies so that you can motivate the person to make improvements in certain areas. When you need to do it, however, always use diplomatic and tactful language, and only focus on issues to do with the individual's performance. Avoid personal attacks.

Reading from the Tone

The vocal attributes play a crucial role in revealing a person's or something about the message that the person wants to portray. For example, a loud voice indicates a person's desire to control and rule over his environment. For example, a drill sergeant uses his voice to intimidate and to dominate. The desire to dominate and tower over others could be indicative of something lacking in the individual's life, and the person is making an effort to compensate for the lack.

One of my best friends is very short, and he speaks deeper and louder than anyone I have ever met. The booming voice, coupled with his need to talk over everyone else is proof of his insecurities. When trying to read into someone, do not just conclude that the person is insecure: it could also be that the person has lost his sense of hearing, or that he is intoxicated. Consider every possible explanation before you come up with a conclusion.

A soft tone could mean some things too. A person who speaks softly does not automatically lack confidence; he could also be fatigued or depressed. A soft voice could say that the person is arrogant because speaking in a hushed voice, you will be forced to listen very keenly to be able to understand what the person is saying. A soft voice could also mean that the person has a calm assurance about himself.

Therefore, in your analysis of persons, think about the reasons behind their tones, mumbling, slow or fast speech, emphasis on some words, emotional tone, or their whining and pretentious tone. Each of them will reveal something more in-depth about the person, besides the face value.

Speech and Body Language

Besides the meanings of the words, both the apparent and the deeper meaning, you need to take note of the verbal gymnastics. For example, you should question why someone is leading you away or towards a particular conversation. Is the person looking for a chance to brag? Is the person compassionate by moving the discussion away from gossiping about another?

The manner in which a person replies to questions in a bid to control the conversation is also suspect. Try to see the reason behind the rumbling, giving a very long answer or a concise answer, changing the subject, or failure to provide any response at all.

In addition, always question any deviations from the norm. A person who rarely uses profane language could be found using it frequently when dealing with a particular group of people. This is indicative of the person's desire to be accepted by trying to present himself as someone he is not.

Words Are a Good Predictor of Health

There has been research to establish the fact that language can be used to determine physical and mental health. The study used data collected from social media platforms. The research was intended to determine how language informs what people can learn about a person from the words they use.

First, the research found that language can be used to predict gender with 92 percent accuracy. This is because women tend to use words like shopping, "love you," birthday, excited, and "yay" while men tend to use profanity in their writing. Men also commonly use words like girlfriend, Xbox, PS3, YouTube, war, and various sports games and personalities.

You can also determine a person's personality type from their social media profile. Extroverts use words like "can't wait," chilling, weekend, party, and girls while introverts favor internet, anime, computer, Pokémon, and others. These results were generated using a computer program, and they are quite applicable to our normal life.

The choice of words was found to hint at a person's mental

health state. Neurotic people tend to post things with the words "hate," "sick of," "bloody," "alone," "stupid," "kill," and "dead." People that are less neurotic mostly focus on sports and religion in their speech and will use phrases like "beautiful day" and "life is good." Other words they use include church, blessed, success, workout, beach and soccer.

People that are highly stressed up talk about their anxiety, pain, fatigue, depression, heartaches, headaches and hurt more often. People that have low-stress levels show some level of enthusiasm about the day and talk about being "pumped" for the day, and what it is likely to bring.

Why is it important to study the words a person uses? Because using the inferences from those words, we can predict a person's personality, and how the said personality influences the individual's behavior.

It is not just the words a person speaks that matter, how they are acted upon matters too, especially if there is a variance between the words and the actions taken. Here are a few secrets you can take up to guide your interaction with others:

- If a person is your competitor, be careful about taking the words he speaks to the heart, they may be geared towards throwing you off your game.
- If a person is speaking to you two ways, saying both yes and no, then believe what he said later and not what was said first. For example, if someone is selling a sweater to you and says that it does not fade, but that if it does, the process takes a long time, believe that the sweater will fade. Make your purchasing decision knowing that it will fade.
- If you want to be friends with someone, or they want to

be your friend or ally, ask as many questions as possible, do not give him the benefit of the doubt.

- When people are just getting to know each other, they use flattery to build a rapport, a friendship, or whatever you could call it, but their true self only comes up later.
- In your interaction with people, you have the liberty of believing whatever it is that you hear. However, you can only trust verifiable statements, such as those said by people you can trust.
- People change, and so do their feelings and priorities. You should only trust a few of those, and ensure that they too trust you.

7

Stop Assuming

No matter how much attention you give towards studying
and analyzing people, you can never really understand
them and their behavior. We know not to judge by appearances,
but even after careful analysis of people and the behaviors they
exhibit, we might still be so far away from analyzing their charac-
ters properly. It is said that the first impressions are lasting
impressions and based on this belief, we rely on the personality
judgments we make immediately after meeting someone for the
first time.

Whether you are looking to start a business with someone, date
someone, or hire them, you need to be sure that these people can
be relied on. You will also want to know whether your personality
can match theirs. However, our decisions are often crowded by
the perceptions we have of them, and although making a snap
judgment about someone seems unfair, this is something we
usually do.

. . .

Sometimes, even finding evidence that suggests something contrary to what you thought before is not enough to shake your first impression. For example, assume that you saw a lady and concluded that she was a lesbian based on her hair, her clothing, and other stereotypes. Later on, you found out that she was dating a man. Would your first impression of her change now that you have contrary information, or would you stick to the first impression?

Life is similar to a box of chocolate, in that you are never too sure of what to expect (of course it's chocolate, just tastes different). We learn how to judge a person based on the beliefs the society has about different kinds of people. These stereotypes could get you to trust a person that you have no business trusting, and blowing off a good person.

The problem now is that the frauds too are aware of these stereotypes also and will camouflage under the pretenses, pretending to be the good kind. For this reason, do not put your trust in people based on society's generalization about a person's behavior and personality. Instead, push these assumptions to the back of your mind and focus on knowing the person at a personal level.

The majority of us were raised not to ask any questions. If we did, we were considered nosy, and rude, and some of us would even get a whooping. Therefore, we grew up knowing that asking questions is wrong because it makes someone feel uncomfortable. Consequently, we tend to depend on what we have heard about something or someone, or at best, rely on our gut feeling to make decisions. In addition, we do not want to put anyone in an uncomfortable space because we want them to like us, and we want to seem polite.

While assumptions and gut feelings have kept many of us out of trouble, a significant proportion has also got into trouble for depending on generalizations and some our sometimes mistaken gut feelings to make decisions. As such, these two methods need a backup plan, in the form of asking questions. You need to assume less and ask more questions.

Making Assumptions About People

When you make assumptions about people, you come up with preconceived notions of who they are, or why they behaved in the manner that they did. You will make assumptions for why a person is late to your appointment, why your mother is not picking your calls, why your partner has not texted you, or why your boss has banged a pile of papers on your desk. Any conclusions reached based on the information you have as at now is incorrect and unfounded. These are all seeds of drama, and they can do nothing better than to distort your life.

The reason we make assumptions is that we are afraid to ask questions. We assume that people think the way we do. The reason for this is that we have grown and the knowledge we have gathered with time has shaped our point of view, and this is what will guide your preconceived notions.

We begin to assume that we have done wr0ng things when someone starts to act cold and distant while it may have nothing to do with us. Someone else could have angered your boss, and he could think that only you would resolve the issue at hand. Therefore, when he bangs the papers on your desk, get to work immediately, and stop wondering what you might have done wrong. Your boss will apologize later, and you can voice your concern about his reaction then.

Take another example, of a female approaching a man and being friendly to him. Besides the important issue they may have talked about, the man will think that the lady is coming on to him. This is a classic example of an assumption, and it is common across different cultures in the world.

The problem with making assumptions is that we tend to believe them. We take them as the new reality, while in fact, these facts only exist in our eyes. The other party will be completely unaware of what you are seeing, and this conflict of ideas could lead to misunderstandings. In the event things go south because we acted on the assumptions, most people defend the assumptions, and now blame other people for the unfortunate consequences.

What's worse is that assumptions are like lies. If you tell one lie, chances are you will tell others to cover up the first one. Behind you, you leave an endless trail of lies. Assumptions are the same way; one leads to another. Once you jump into conclusions (maybe confusion?) about one thing, you are likely to jump into others along the way. The result is that you lose touch with reality tremendously.

. . .

The way out of a mess like that is to have facts. Refer to them and do not make assumptions.

Things That We Can Safely Assume About People

Extroversion/Introversion

The person you are dealing with will either have an outgoing personality or be shy. This kind of personality type is easy to determine, even in the first 10 seconds of meeting a person. You will know this by the person's body language, excitement in the voice, eye contact, hand gestures, and animated facial expressions. All these cues will tell you how socially comfortable a person is, which is common among extroverted people. People who are not sociable are introverted.

Attraction

In the culture of internet dating, you can tell whether you like someone just by looking at their appearance. You already know whether you are attracted to brunettes, blondes, black people or others. You already know what will work for you and what will not. You are likely to be attracted to someone who is similar to you, and you will consider a person like that to be more attractive than the rest of the pack.

Competence

One researcher, Alex Todorov, conducted a study to see the response that people gave to faces and found that subjects considered people with wrinkles at their eyes and thin lips to be intelligent, go-getters and distinguished. People with baby faces were deemed to be naïve, submissive and weird, although this same group was thought to be warm, honest and kind.

Openness

Within 10 seconds of meeting someone, his body language should tell you whether he is open or not. If the person is receptive to you, his arms will be relaxed, his feet will point in your direction, the shoulders will be pulled back, and the head will be up. He will maintain eye contact, and the expressions in his face will be happy.

When a person is not receptive to you, his body language will be turned inwards. His arms will be crossed, he will avoid eye contact, and his facial expressions will be disagreeable.

Neuroticism

From face value, you will have an idea about a person's germophobic behavior like fidgeting, personal hygiene, avoiding a handshake, and even repetitive behavior like whether the person bites his nails. You may assume that someone indicating this behavior suffers from anxiety, even if the fear is not apparent by any other signs.

How Assumptions Affect the Other Party

Have you been in a position where someone assumed things about you that were far from the truth? Most likely, the person did not even know you enough or did not take time to confirm the assumptions with you or with someone that knows you. The result is that the person feels so hurt upon realizing the false, now accusations, that have been made against him or her.

You must have seen it on TV, where a couple is continually fighting because one party makes assumptions over the other. See it on Divorce Court. Partners go to the show ready to end their relationships because the other has become insecure and has started making unfounded assumptions against the other. Watching all this drama even gets the audience worked up, let alone the partner about whom the premises have been made.

A friend recently shared with me the reasons for his recent breakup with a long-time girlfriend. The lady kept making assumptions about him that were false majority of the time. The man would get angry and not respond to the wild unfounded accusations. After a while though, the man got tired of it all and ended the relationship. The lady realized the mistake she had made, but by then, it was too late.

The assumptions you make about a person tells him the opinion you have of him. If the assumptions are demeaning, the person will feel belittled and disrespected. If the assumptions are good, the person will feel honored, and it will even boost his esteem. Everyone wants to be treated like an object of admiration, especially by people that they just met, who know nothing about the person's past. This is the reason people move away when they want to start a new life.

Therefore, instead of making assumptions that could irreparably damage a person's ego, why not ask questions you may have? A person will feel more validated shaping your perception of him than when he has to fight with the unfounded beliefs you have of him.

Assumptions Influence Your Reality

Buddha said that it is impossible for your worst enemy to hurt you to the extent that your thoughts would do. Majority of the assumptions we make do not lead to happy endings. Think of the assumptions you would make about a blind date that fitted a particularly negative stereotype. You assumed that the person was a fraud and was only there to catfish you. You begin seeing the new business that you just started collapsing. All these are negative assumptions, and they lead to a cynical mind altogether. Things could be going so well and all of a sudden, someone begins to think of how a disaster would come up and destroy everything around them.

The ideas you have in your head come courtesy of your subconscious mind, and the good thing is that you can reprogram it to come up with more positive thoughts. You do this by deactivating all negative ideas and replacing them with positive ones that will uplift you.

Here are a few steps to take to reprogram your subconscious mind successfully:

- **Feed your mind with positive things:** Once you realize that a contrary idea has planted itself in your mind, take it out and replace it with a positive one. Instead of seeing your business collapse or wondering where the next disaster will come, think about how everything could go well. Your business could start making profits again, and you could get to enjoy your peace without having to deal with any disasters and problems.

- **Be aware and ask questions:** Every time you experience a negative emotion or a positive one about someone, try to think of where that thought could have originated. Check to see that the source of the emotion you felt is valid.

- **Associate with positive people:** If you meet a person whose speech is always negative, keep off that person. You would not be walking away based on assumptions because you already have evidence that the person is spreading negativity in your life. Accommodate the people with whom you share values and those that love you for who you are.

- **Keep the environment that you are in positive:** Ensure that the stimuli that surround you are positive and uplifting. Instead, 0f meeting with friends at a bar where people have to yell to be heard and where all manner of dangers can occur, go out with your friends for dinner and take some alcohol there, if you must. The cordial atmosphere at a restaurant will allow you to connect with them better than you would at a bar.

- **Changing all negative aspects of your life into positive ones will require attention and practice.** However, once you have made these changes, you will begin to notice that the positivity will influence positive changes in your life.

Asking and Not Guessing

Making inquiries sets you up for a deeper understanding and clarity. It means that you need to stop being passive and letting things play as they will, and instead, be actively engaged in managing the affairs that surround your life.

If you set your mind on making assumptions, you will assume that your partner wants to marry you just because he gave you a key to his apartment. You will assume that you are about to be promoted just because your responsibilities were added. However, the best way to step out of the assumptions is to ask questions. Ask your partner whether he is open to marriage. Ask your boss whether you are up for a promotion.

The minute you realize that you are in the assumptions zone, ask yourself what evidence you have that things are as they appear. Until you have yourself a ring, do not assume that you are about to get married. This is also the case for those seeking a promotion. Until you receive your letter of appointment or your boss calls you into his office to notify you of the same, do not assume that the promotion is here yet. Keep working hard to get it.

Here are some tricks to shield you from assumptions:

- **When passing essential information, repeat what you say thrice, and ask questions.** If you are delegating tasks, discussing terms of a deal with someone, or engaging in other things like these, do not assume that the person will understand what you are saying from the word go. Repeat yourself, at least thrice, to ensure that the instructions the person is giving are clear, and once you are done with that, seek to know whether the person has understood everything you had to say. You do not want to find out that the person did something completely different weeks later.

- **You also need to keep with you a constant reminder to avoid assumptions**. For example, you could write one or two post-it notes to remind yourself to cut the assumptions and instead did deeper into things. If someone comes to you and claims that he or she works with a particular company, don't take his or her word for it; go ahead and confirm. Any verifiable details about people you are interacting with should be sought so that you be sure that you are dealing with a genuine person, whose details you know.

- **Take up is the habit of validation**. If you make an assumption don't stop at that, verify that assumption with facts. For example, if you are thinking or starting a business with someone, validate your choice of him as the right business partner and not the large number of options that you have. If you are looking to start a business or to start producing a product, validate the need for what you are introducing into the market before you invest and start making losses.

8

The Process of Interpreting Behavior

Perception and Interpretation

Interpretation of behavior is the third stage of perception. Perception refers to the set of unconscious processes a person goes through to make sense of the sensations and stimuli the individual encounters. Your perception is based on your interpretation of the various sensations and the impressions you get from the stimuli that you get from the world around you. Perception is what helps you navigate the world because it guides your decision-making process, from what to eat for breakfast, the clothes to wear, the relationship to be in and the reaction you give to something dangerous that is coming your way.

If you close your eyes and try to remember the details in the room you are in, do you remember the color of the walls? Do you recall the location of the furniture there? Do you remember the angle that the shadows make? Whatever you can or cannot remember is guided by your perception. Your brain cannot remember everything it encounters; you will only take note of some things, guided by your perception.

The difference in perception of one person from another is best illustrated by an optical illusion where if you and your friend look at the illusion, you are likely to note one thing, while your friend will note something entirely different. The difference is brought by the variation in the processes that the brain goes through to create your reaction or perception of stimuli. These processes are selection, organization, and interpretation.

This is the last stage of perception; it is the stage in which a person subjectively considers and understand stimuli. This is the stage in which we attach meaning to what we see.

Interpretation is influenced by experiences, beliefs, cultural values, self-concept, needs, expectations, involvement, and other individual influences. Experience plays a primary role in under-standing behavior. For example, a person who has gone through physical abuse might interpret a person raising his hand towards them as someone who wants to hit him or her. On the other hand, a person with a sports background could interpret the same gesture as someone leaning in for a high-five, and he will raise his hand too.

Culture provides a structure, rules, expectations, and guidelines to govern behavior. Based on these variations, you will note that people understand, interpret and respond to behavior in different ways. For example, Americans mothers are known for celebrating their children's successes, however slight. Chinese mothers are known for their focus on discipline. Based on this difference, what would appear to the Chinese mother as a lack of discipline, an American mother might interpret as basic childhood curiosity and exploration.

Self-concept is also a crucial influence on the viewpoint a person has. Self-concept refers to the pool of thoughts and beliefs a person has about himself in regard to his racial identity, sexuality, intelligence, and others. If you believe that you are an attractive person, you will likely interpret stares you get from other people as admiration for your beauty. However, if you think you are unattractive, you will consider the stares to be negative judgment.

Desire and expectations can determine how you interpret stimuli. An individual's desire to avoid the negative stimuli causes him or her to interpret stimuli in a particular way.

The role of schemata

Interpretation of behavior is a conscious and deliberate event in which a person attaches meaning to the experiences he has had using mental structures called schemata. Schemata can be likened to databases that store the information that you use when you interpret new experiences. All of us have schemata, and they are different because of the variations in the experiences we have gone through over time. The bits of information from each event combines with bits from other incidents resulting in a complex web of information.

For example, you have an overall schema in regard to how you interpret education due to the experiences you have had in school when interacting with teachers and other students. The schema started forming even before you entered school based on the information you got about the school from your parents, your siblings, and the images you saw from different forms of media.

For example, you learned that a ruler, a notebook and a pen are associated with the learning environment. With time, you found out about new concepts like recess, grades, homework, taking tests and studying. You also developed relationships with your classmates, teachers, janitors, and administrators. As your education progressed, so did your schema.

The ease or the difficulty of revising or re-evaluating a schema varies from one person to another, and from one situation to another. For example, some students do not experience any problems changing their schemas as they move from one education level to another, even as their expectations of academic and behavior engagement change. Others do not have a smooth transition because they experience problems interpreting new information using the old yet incompatible schema.

Most of us have been in situations like these when we encountered mistakes, frustrations and disappointments revising our schemas but we eventually learned how to do it right. Being able to adapt your schema is a sign of cognitive complexity and cognitive growth, which is an essential part of life. Therefore, even if a person encounters challenges and makes mistakes, it is alright because the person is in the process of learning and growing.

Being aware of your schemata is important because your interpretation determines how you behave. For example, if you are leading a group discussion and you notice that one of the members is shy, you will instinctively avoid asking him to speak based on your schema about how shy people do not like to talk in public or that they make poor public speakers.

Schemata also guide your interactions and become a script that guides your behaviors. For example, you know how to act on a first date, at a waiting room, in a classroom and even at a game show. A person who has never been in any of these environments will know how to behave.

Schemata are also used to interpret other people's behavior and to form impressions about who they are. This process is aided by soliciting information about the said persons so that we can place the people in a particular schema. For example, in the United States and many other cultures of the West, the identity of a person is closely tied to what the person does for a living. In an introduction, one of the first thing we say about ourselves, or about others is the kind of work we do.

The conversation you have with a person will shift depending on the title the person introduced to you has. For example, the conversation you have with a doctor is different from that which you have with an artist. We often make similar distinctions based on a person's gender, culture, and other factors that could influence perception.

In summary, the schemata guide our interpretation of people, individuals, things, and places, which filters the information and perception we have before, during and after an interaction. The schemata are stored in our memories and are retrieved whenever we need to interpret behavior, and all other stimuli around us. Just like apps are updated when a new version is created, the schemata are updated as we encounter new experiences in life.

The Attribution Theory of Interpreting Behavior

In the field of psychology, the word attribution is used to refer to the judgment you make concerning another person's behavior. Therefore, the attribution theory is meant to explain the process of attribution, which is the process of understanding the reasons behind particular behavior.

To shed light on the attribution concept, imagine that your girlfriend has canceled in the plans you had to meet up for a coffee date. Will you just assume that some unavoidable event came up or will you think that your girlfriend is avoiding you? Said in other words, will you assume that this behavior was situational (caused by external circumstances) or will you assume that it was dispositional (brought by the person's inherent traits)? The answer you give is the basis for studying attribution.

Psychologist Fritz Heider examined how individuals conclude whether a particular behavior is externally or internally generated. According to him, the behavior is determined by motivation and capacity. Capacity refers to a person's ability to enact a particular behavior, which is the determination of whether our innate traits and the environment we are in can allow the behavior we want to portray. On the other hand, motivation relates to our intentions and the amount of effort we want to portray.

Heider concluded that a person needs both motivation and capacity to portray particular behavior. For example, your ability to participate in a marathon depends on your physical fitness and your desire to push through the race.

Some of the most popular attribution theories are Weiner's three-dimensional model, Kelly's covariation model and the correspondent inference theory.

Weiner's Three-Dimensional Model

Bernard Weiner, in this theory, suggested that people examine behavior based on three dimensions, which include stability, locus, and controllability.

Locus refers to the determination of whether external or internal factors cause behavior. Controllability refers to a person's ability to change the course of the outcome of an event by increasing the effort he is using. Stability refers to the likelihood that the behavior will happen again.

Weiner suggested that the attributions people make also affect the emotions they feel. For example, people are more likely to feel proud if they think that their innate characteristics like talent, and not the external factors like luck, have caused them to succeed.

Kelly's Covariation Model

Harold Kelley claimed that people rely on three kinds of information when trying to decide whether the behavior a person has portrayed was motivated internally or externally. We use distinctiveness, consensus, and consistency.

Distinctiveness is the determination of whether a person will act similarly in other environments. If a person only acts a certain way in a particular situation, then his behavior will only be attributed to that situation and not to the person.

The consensus is the determination of whether other people would act the same way if they were placed in a similar situation. If other people are likely to behave in the same way, then the behavior does not indicate the individual's unique innate characteristics.

Consistency refers to whether a person would act the same way, in the same situation, every time the event occurs. If the behavior observed is different from one time to the next, then it is difficult to attribute specific behavior to the individual.

Based on this analysis, whenever the levels of consensus, distinctiveness, and consistency are high, the behavior is attributed to the situation.

Let's see this in an example. Imagine your husband John likes muffins so much. All of your other friends also like cupcakes (high consensus), John likes all kinds of pastries (high distinctiveness) and that John has loved all kinds of muffins he has ever tried (high consistency). The information we have here suggests that your husband John's behavior of liking muffins is the result of a specific situation or circumstance (muffins are generally liked), and not because John inherently loves cupcakes.

In cases where the consensus level is low, the distinctiveness level is low, but the consistency level is high, then we can conclude that the behavior is particular to the person.

Let's see another example. Suppose you want to see which of your children would want to go camping with you and you find out that none of your other children liked their camping experiences (low consensus). However, Mary loves all kinds of outdoor activities (low distinctiveness) and has always had fun in the scout camps she attended (high consistency). The information you have got will tell you that your children do not like camping, but Mary. Mary's love for camping is inherent because she likes many outdoor activities. It is likely that your other children went camping against their will.

Correspondent Inference Theory

The correspondent inference theory is the work of Keith Davis and Edward Jones. The theory suggests that if a person behaves in a way that is socially desirable, you cannot infer much about that person. For example, if you borrow your friend his pencil and he hands it to you, you cannot infer much about the friend's character because many people would have acted in that same way in a similar situation. However, if you borrow the pencil and your friend refuses to let you have his pencil, you are likely to make an inference about his character because it is not in line with the socially desirable response.

The theory also suggests that not much about an individual's internal motivation can be inferred if the individual is acting in line with a particular social role. For example, the job description of a salesperson or a receptionist requires him or her to be outgoing and friendly in the job context. Since this behavior is a requirement at work, you cannot then start saying that the outgoing personality and the friendliness are a part of that individual's innate traits.

Reasons Behavioral Interpretation Could Go Wrong

People are prone to biases that affect or cloud rational thinking and the accurate interpretation of behavior. The underlying reason for this is limited exposure because people's interpretation of motives is based on experience and intuition. The more a person observes behavior, the better he will be at interpreting behavior. However, things could still go wrong due to the following five reasons:

People interpret behavior based on personal perspectives

Most people believe that their ideas are always right. For example, a person will have an opinion and colorful names to give to people who drive faster or slower than them believing that his speed is the right one. Consequently, people evaluate other people's behavior based on their own. A comparison like this leads to flawed judgment and a lack of compassion.

Different motives could drive similar behavior

Experience and observing behavior may prove insufficient because different motives may sometimes drive similar behavior. Besides, people tend to react differently to the same stimuli.

The motive is always tied to the personality

Although character and personality endure longer than situational motives, most times, individuals assume that personality traits can effectively explain motivation intent. The fact is that personality may sometimes be used to foretell how a person will react under particular circumstances, but the integrative nature of motivation may counter the predictability of personality. Sometimes, there will be factors that will override typical behavior patterns such as when an introvert becomes the life of the party.

Many people do not understand their own motives

Interpreting motives is distorted because unlike the physical attributes, preferences, beliefs, and dispositions cannot be examined directly. Even more complicated is the fact that we assess other people's m0tives based on the behavior and information we have received from others or how people portray themselves publicly.

The problem with this analysis, however, is that most people do not behave in public as they do in private, which further complicates motive interpretation. The aspect of social desirability further complicates the analysis, which means that some behaviors will be more acceptable culturally than others. It is also true that some people deliberately change their behavior to meet societal expectations.

Emotions disrupt or disguise normal behavior

Guided by emotions, it is easy to misinterpret motives. When people are emotionally stained, their response patterns change. Sometimes, the mind will succumb to the perception of stress, pressure, strain, discomfort, and happiness, and inevitably, their normal psychological and physiological patterns are distorted by the prevailing emotions. Accurate interpretation of behavior needs you to realize that environmental factors will always be interpreted subjectively, which activates different kinds of emotions among the people. Positive emotions can lead an individual to go out and look for a target, while negative emotions lead to avoidance.

9

There Goes the Lie

You will be surprised to learn that more than 80% of the lies people tell go undetected. However, when you think back to your childhood, you wouldn't be surprised that lies are so prevalent. Many of us lied to the tooth about virtually everything we did: we stole and ate candy before dinner, fell the lampshade, let the dog out of the house without a leash, and so many other wrong things. The issue with lying is that it reduces the possibility of receiving punishment if the lie goes through. The thrill of not getting into trouble encourages lying among children and becomes the foundation of more lies told as the individual grows up.

Techniques You Should Use to Spot A Lie

Although people get away with many lies, you may be able to spot most of them if you learn how to identify the signs. Below are some techniques you can apply to determine whether the individual is telling the truth:

. . .

Begin by asking neutral questions

Asking neutral nonthreatening questions helps the person to become comfortable. In this comfort, be on guard so that you identify the baseline of the conversation. See how the person behaves when answering questions that have nothing to do with him. For example, you can start by asking questions about the weather, the person's weekend plans, family life, their job, or any other issue you are sure would elicit a comfortable response.

When the person is responding, ensure that you also observe his eye movement, and body language so that you know how this two shift when the person is telling the truth. Does the person keep glancing side to side or does he maintain eye contact? Does he keep shifting his posture? Make sure that you have a list of warm-up questions so that as the person answers them, you will have observed a trend.

Shift to the "hot" conversation

By now, you are ready to shift from the neutral territory to the lie zone. When you do that, you should be able to observe a significant change in eye movement, facial expressions, sentence structure and other kinds of body language. However much the individual is in control of his reactions, he will still give some clues subconsciously when he shifts to lying. This is the reason why the first step, that of establishing a baseline of normal behavior is important before entering the lying sphere.

Look out for micro-expressions

A person who is lying will not lack a facial expression that can give him away; the problem is that some of the expressions are subtle and spotting them can be a challenge. However, here's what you should look out for: some people's facial coloration will change, and they will adopt a slight pink shade, some bite their lip, some people's nostrils flare slightly, others blink rapidly while some people will have slight perspiration on their faces.

It is particularly challenging to hide emotions because unlike body language; you cannot be in full control of what appears on your face. One study found that secrets were more likely revealed when people put on a false face by inhibiting or faking different kinds of emotions. This is because the emotions will leak through tiny cracks that last about a fifth of a second, and they will reveal the true emotions the person is feeling such as guilt and anger.

Experts want that the signs of emotion do not necessarily indicate guilt, but they will give you a peek into the emotions that the individual is trying to conceal. However, whichever expression you see, follow it up with some questions, and find out the reason behind those feelings and emotions.

Monitor the body language

When lying, most people pull their body inward to make themselves less noticeable and to feel smaller. They want to hide or disappear, and the only way their brains can achieve that is by creating the illusion that the person is small or minute. Other liars become squirmy and will sometimes conceal their hands to hide their fidgeting fingers. Some even begin to shrug their shoulders.

The tone, the cadence, and the structuring of sentences

Have you ever noticed that when you lie, your tone changes? So does the cadence of your speech. A liar does the same and starts speaking more quickly than normal or even more slowly. The tone will also be higher, or lower. Most of the time, the structure of the sentences becomes more complicated because the brain will be working twice as much to keep up with the creation of the tale, and to control the expressions the person makes.

Of importance, however, is to realize that every person behaves differently when lying. As such, it is best to begin by learning the person's baseline behavior so that you take note of any changes that the person will register.

The person starts taking himself out of the story

A liar thrives by keeping himself or herself out of trouble. Therefore, to avoid any repercussions of whatever lie he is telling, the liar will slowly start removing himself from the story, and start turning the attention towards other people. The I's, and Me's will decrease significantly. The liar does that so that you can psychologically begin to distance him from the story and actually consider him a friend.

Look out for stress signs

Let's say that you are sure that the individual you have been speaking to, your child, your boss, or your friend, has lied to you. You decide to press them for some clarification in regard to the statement they've made. The chances are that you will put the person in a position to give you a clue that will let you in on the discomfort.

You may notice changes in their body movement, temperature rise, and increased perspiration. This is because the basal and limbic ganglia systems are the ones that control stress and make visible the nonverbal deception that the human being exhibits.

Most people do not know that when the brain is stressed, the temperature in the brain rises, and this is often indicated by perspiration around the top of the head or on the upper lip region. Some people begin to touch their face. This habit acts as a pacifier and produces a calming effect on the stressed brain.

Of course, all these signs depend on the baseline behavior you have established because some people will exhibit the behavior you think is synonymous with lying. Some naturally have developed a habit of touching their faces or twirling their hairs.

Notice the fake smile

Liars trying to conceal their emotions are more likely to press their lips together leaving a forced or a tense smile. However, do not just check the lips, monitor the mouth/eye combination.

· · ·

A person telling the truth will engage his entire face in the smile. Remember the famous Mona Lisa? Crow's feet are a sign of dishonesty.

Although you may be tempted to distrust a person who is a little shifty-eyed or a person who breaks eye contact, or even one who cannot stomach looking at you directly, there could be many innocent reasons for this behavior. Some people are naturally nervous, shy and socially awkward. Therefore, focusing on the eyes alone could have you making the wrong conclusion. Instead, use the combination of eyes and the smile to come up with a definite judgment.

Whenever you think that someone is forcing a smile, think along the lines of the following emotions: fear, sadness, surprise, anger, contempt, disgust and happiness. These emotions are likely to be what underlies the fake smile.

Considering the "blended" expression, think of the lower half of the face indicating secondary human emotion while the upper half shows the primary emotion. Therefore, a real smile will be seen in both the upper and lower hemispheres of the face, and when they match, you can conclude that the person is genuinely happy. A fake smile will have a disconnect between the two hemispheres because while the mouth may be smiling, the eyes will exhibit anger, contempt or disgust.

Questions You Should Answer to Know if the Person is Lying

The following questions require a YES or No response. Answer them to the best of your ability to establish whether the individual is lying.

Does the person stand to gain if you buy into the statement?

People are more likely to lie if they expect to get something out of being believed. For example, a politician will make all kinds of promises so that the people may elect him. A salesperson will also associate the product he is selling with all sorts of benefits to make a sale.

Will the person lose if I uncover the statements said to be untrue?

The majority of the people are less likely to tell lies if when the truth is revealed, they stand to lose important ongoing relationships. For example, a person you just met at a club does not care about lying to you because you two do not have any significant relationship and you are less likely to see each other in the future. Conversely, a business owner who is counting on establishing a relationship with his customers is less likely to tell lies in his interaction with customers.

Is what you hear too good to be true?

Anyone who tells you exactly what you wanted to hear is most likely lying.

. . .

Will the source gain if you do not believe the statement he says?

If the person tells you an uncomfortable truth that he or she has struggled to say, especially one that would not be less pleasant if you didn't believe it, then it is likely that that statement is true.

For example, a friend who admits to having done something stupid at the club is likely to be telling the truth.

Is the source capable of answering drill questions?

When it comes to lies, and many other issues in life, the devil is in the details. Many liars come up with top-level lies. However, if you open a line of questioning, you are likely to discover black spots and inconsistencies in the stories.

For example, most companies that produce water indicate that they use ozonation, reverse osmosis, and ultraviolet rays to purify their water. However, most of these words are only marketing lingo. If you asked a company rep what they mean by that, which I did, the person could not even come up with a complete sentence.

Are there reliable independent sources to collaborate with the story?

Any information that you can only get from one source only has most likely made up. A credible source must have a reliable independent source that collaborates the story. Many conspiracy theorists cannot provide support for their stories.

Is the person wealthy and influential?

This question may seem unnecessary, but surprisingly, it has been proven that wealthy people are more prone to stealing, cheating and lying more than those who are not wealthy. This is mostly observed among politicians and other wealthy people in society.

Does the information you receive assume causality?

Just become one event happened after another does not mean that the first event caused the second event. Liars depend on coincidences like this one to justify their stories and create a false causality. Many of them could just be confused; however, they may not even be aware that what they are propagating is a lie.

Are weasel words shielding the truth?

Most liars will shield their false information with clever weasel words that introduce some level of deniability. They will make statements that have some truth but couch the true statements with words that will cause the hearers to misinterpret the information.

For example, the liar will say, "Dentists recommend brushing your teeth twice a day with Colgate for healthy gums and teeth."

By this statement, the person is saying a true statement(the need to brush your teeth twice a day), but he or she includes the word

Colgate, and it is likely that the dentists did not make that specification.

Does the statement include averages?

The "average" concept only makes sense when used to compare things that are similar to the GPA. When used in statements describing things that vary widely, the term can be quite confusing.

For example saying that if you put one billionaire and 999 homeless people, the average wealth of the people in the room will be $1 million is just impractical.

Does the person have all the answers?

While answering your questions should not be suspect, you should keep an eye out for how the answer is given. When you ask a person a question like "Where were you this weekend?" The person may pause a little to think before giving you the answer. However, when an individual is lying, he will have rehearsed the answers to any questions you may have. Therefore, when you begin to ask the questions, expects to be shot at with ready answers. The person will not have any form of hesitation.

If a person has immediate answers to every question you ask without hesitation, consider this a dead giveaway that the person had rehearsed quite adequately.

. . .

Is the person going too far lengths to prove his honesty?

When a person is truthful, he is not worried that you may not believe him. When a person uses phrases like, "To be honest…" or "I swear to you that I am not lying…" these could be clues that the person is lying through the teeth. An honest person will not feel the need to convince you that he or she is honest.

Does the person overly use the verb "would?"

For some strange reason, people who are lying insert the word "would" or "wouldn't" many times, in their speech. For example, while an honest weight lifter at the gym would say, "I do not use any performance-enhancing drugs like steroids," a doping weight lifter will say, "I would never use performance enhancing drugs like steroids." Difference? Once word

Does the person struggle or even show the need to find the right words?

Some people naturally take some time to choose the words to say in comparison to others. Still, they do not do this all the time. For most people, there is barely a time to find the right words because they are stressed and want to put their point across, or they are excited and want to talk about the good news some more.

Therefore, when watching out for this point, consider also the context in which the words are spoken. Once you identify the "normal" speech baseline, now go ahead and spot the lies.

. . .

If you award one point to every question that you answer "Yes" to, then the higher the score, the more likely that it is a lie.

If you learn to keep your attention on what people are saying and how they are saying it, by taking note of the factors listed above, your ability to spot and identify liars will increase, and it will be very difficult to dupe you. Whether you are dealing with your toddler who denies everything, your teenager trying to get out 0f punishment or a fully-fledged pathological liar, your radar will be so highly raised that you can notice a liar a mile away, in your interactions, at least.

10

Identifying a Romantic Interest

Finding the right romantic partner, both for the women and the men, requires careful analysis and assessment of your options. Although sometimes it proves difficult to know for sure whether someone has a romantic interest in you, being certain of it will make it easier for you to determine your next move. Whether the person in question is a casual acquaintance or a long-time friend, paying watching out for the telltale signs of a romantic attraction is the first step closer to either you or them making a move and revealing his or her true feelings.

To assess the viability of a romantic interest, take the following steps:

First, evaluate the amount of eye contact the other party gives you. The number of times and the intensity will reveal whether the person has developed romantic feelings for you. Actions too will provide you with a clue. For example, does he or she scan your entire body during your interactions, or does he keep sneaking glances at you during the day? If he does, it means that you have become the object of his romantic thoughts.

The second step is to examine the individual's body in the course of your interactions. Realize that although verbal communication is essential, non-verbal communication is a critical element in indicating an attraction. Some of the confirmatory signs you will see include the person seeking opportunities to touch your skin, or the person leaning in closer when you speak to him in an attempt to take in every word you say. The person might even begin to mirror what you do, which should tell you that he is open to relating with you at a personal level.

The third thing you do is to assess the amount of attention the person gives to you. Look out for how the person reacts when you dish about your personal life. For example, he will get visibly upset when you talk about the good times you had with someone else, or he could seek more information about your interests, hobbies, and goals in life. If the man is equally open to talking to you about himself, his interests, what he intends to do with his life, his goals and ambitions, then you should rest assured that he is interested in you. The man will also enjoy engaging in thought-provoking subjects with you.

The fourth thing you should do is to pay attention to the efforts the individual puts in his desire to please you. Actions like this may range from simple things like pulling out a chair for you to sit, to incredible acts like changing his entire wardrobe to satisfy a lazy comment you made, possibly about how you like your man to dress.

You should also keep track of the compliments the new interest pays you because they will reveal to you how you are in his eyes. For example, he may say that you look like you can make a good mother or wife, which will mean that he sees the potential in you to become a wife and a mother, which he admires greatly.

Signs That a Man Has a Romantic Interest in You

The section above has approached romantic interest from a general perspective but used the "he" pronoun. Based on that reading, you already have an idea about how men express their interest.

This section briefly states some other signs that indicate that a man is interested in a woman:

Getting jealous easily

If his romantic interest has another guy around her or she is flirting with another guy, he quickly gets offended. The girl might not be his yet, but he sure is working on it.

Telling the woman that he wants her

If a man tells a woman that he is interested in her, he is. It is the most obvious way he can communicate his interest. If he has managed to put it in words, it must be true.

Listening to what she has to say

A guy who wants a woman will make every effort to listen to everything she has to say. He will appear interested even in things that he would normally never be caught doing like talking about the latest celebrity couple, discussing recipes and other things that guys don't care about usually.

Can't take his eyes off her

The man is mesmerized by the woman, and because of this, he is unable to keep his eyes off of her. By looking at her, he is keeping watch of her every move and behavior, trying to know more about her. On the other hand, he will be on the lookout for any other potential men that would have their eyes on his chosen woman.

Improving his appearance

As a guy studies what his potential woman likes, he will change different aspects about himself to look attractive to her. First on his agenda will be his appearance. He will change his wardrobe, go in for a better haircut and maintain good hygiene to makes sure that he catches the lady's attention. When a man is willing to move to such great lengths, he is definitely interested.

Enlisting help from friends to set-up for a date

When a guy starts introducing a girl to his friends, he is doing that hoping that she will stick around for a while. It is also a way of marking his territory to ensure that his friends will not start pursuing you.

Personal space no longer matters

Guys will choose body language any day over gushing at you with their words. Although a guy like this will tell you what you want to hear, his priority is body language. A guy who likes you will invade your personal space by closing in on the distance between you two to the point of touching you.

He is present

A man will not spend time with a woman unless he is her good friend, or that he wants her. Once he is interested, he will make all sorts of excuses to spend some more time with her. He may even give up some the time he spends with his guy friends to be with her.

Identifying Romantic Interest in a Woman

It is difficult to tell if a female friend you have known for a long time or even just recently would want to take your friendship to the next level.

Traditionally, men are the ones that make the first move, push their date towards giving that first kiss and make an effort towards the initiation of higher levels of intimacy with women. All this responsibility can put pressure on a man making it difficult for him to make the first move. However, research shows that women are the ones who signal whether the man can go ahead and initiate the whole love process or not.

Having realized that, what nonverbal signals do women indicate to let the other person know that they have developed a romantic interest?

Body language

If this is a friend you have known a while, try to see whether she hugs you tightly or whether she hands you the single-hand hug as though you are unwanted. If a woman is interested in you, she will cuddle you and hug you for a longer time. She will spend an unusual amount of time gazing into your eyes, and when you meet her on the road or in the hallways, she will flash you that secret smile.

Suppose she has developed a romantic interest at a stranger at a restaurant, in the classroom or any other place that a love interest would develop, her behavior changes slightly from when dealing with a friend. Her secret weapon will be her gaze.

The woman will maintain an extended gaze at the man she deems attractive, and keep at it until the man takes notice of her. When he does, she will smile, break the gaze, turn back to the gaze, smile again then break the gaze again. (It's a lot, I know).

Another strategy she will use is to pimp herself. She will go two extra miles to look great in preparation for meeting the man she in whom has an interest. She will fix her hair, take up an open body posture (where the arms are kept away from the body) or will orient her body to face the man.

Once the man approaches her, which most men always do, both parties orient their bodies towards each other, and the woman may continue engaging in her seductive behavior like self-touching, palming (opening up her palm and wrist and displaying them) and leaning back to expose her neck.

. . .

If you suspect that your female friend, possibly one you have known for a long time, is showing the body language signs discussed, the next time you meet her, grab her suddenly and pull her towards yourself. Bring her so close that you can feel how her body reacts, such as a racing heartbeat or increased breathing. If she remains right there and does not jerk away, and her pupils dilate in anticipation of the next move, lean over and kiss her.

Her time

A woman interested in you will go out of her way to make time for you no matter how tight her schedule is. Perhaps she has recently started making excuses to meet you every other day. If indeed she has, this confirms that she is interested in pursuing a romantic relationship with you.

A lady will continuously seek to spend more time with a man she likes. For example, if she chooses to spend Friday night with you instead of accompanying her friends, she likes you, certainly.

Joins and likes your company

You should know that a lady likes you if she shows signs that she enjoys your company immensely. She will laugh heartily at your jokes, even the dry ones. When she is feeling down, you are the first person she will call. This is also what she will do when she is excited about something. Whenever she feels like she has been maltreated, she will call you to complain, possibly suggesting that she sees you as a source of security, both emotionally and physically. By the time you end your conversation, she will be jolly again and her spirit lifted.

. . .

A lady will ask you to accompany her to public places like social events, because she wants to flaunt you to other people, to introduce you to her family if you haven't met them already, and to take pictures with you. Whenever you spend time with her, time seems to fly, and she keeps asking you to come back another time.

Jealousy

Jealousy is one of the protective gears a lady has towards the man for whom she has struck an interest. Surprisingly, a woman will be attracted to a man who already has a lady in his arms but will not want to share him once she gets him. A woman who wants you to herself will demand that you treat her differently and especially from how you treat other women in your life. If you show interest in another woman or do as much as hold a hand, the girl that is into you will sulk all day, block your calls and not talk to you until you own up to your mistake and apologize.

If you are hanging out with your friends and a lady seated across from you likes you, notice how your eyes will lock every time. If she is sitting next to a guy, she will want to hold him tighter to see how you react, whether you get jealous or not.

Confides in you

Once a lady has liked you, she will tell you all kinds of intimate details about herself, and the troubles surrounding her work and her family. She will also let you in on her fears. She will seek to know your opinion regarding various issues, from how her character comes off, her dressing, politics, her career, to the state of the economy. With time, you two will connect so well that your conversations will feel like heart-to-heart mumblings.

See how her friends treat you

How the girl's close friends treat you should hint to you how she feels about you. If you will be hanging out and then they excuse themselves to allow you two some quiet time, or in between conversations they joke that you two would make a cute couple, know that she absolutely likes you.

On the contrary, if they act bored whenever you are around, excuse themselves or ignore you entirely, know that you do not mean anything to their friend. Some will even be bold enough to let you know the truth, to your face. In a case like this, run for your life and don't look back.

Considers you special

A woman that likes you will occasionally bend some of her principles and rules to accommodate you. She would never do these things for other men. For example, she will spend days that are important to her with you. She will stay by your side taking care of you when you catch the flu. She will leave hints at your house such as a toothbrush or an item of clothing. She will also wear your perfume. All these she will do with the hope that you see it, and somehow reciprocate the special treatment.

Tries to make you a better version of yourself

Once a lady has confirmed your eligibility as her mate, she starts working towards helping you become your ideal self. For example, she will start talking you out of your self-destructive habits like excessive alcohol intake, untidiness, or skipping classes. She will urge you to become more responsible, to clean up your house and to take your studies or your job more seriously. She will suggest a haircut that would augment your look.

Overall, a lady who likes you will want to help you become a better man because she envisions that you will be her husband.

Signs That You Have Developed a Romantic Interest

Starting to like someone is different for everyone. Some people recognize the feeling immediately while others are not so sure, or brush it off as infatuation. In both cases, however, your body will step in and let you know whether the feeling is thereby leaving you some not so subtle signs that you like someone. These signs include:

Can't stop staring at the person

Eye contact is a sign that you are fixated on something. Therefore, if you can't stop staring at someone, he or she is your fixation.

Getting a "high" feeling

When you are interested in someone, it is natural to feel like you are out of your mind. A study found that when you like someone, your brain behaves as it does when you are high on cocaine. This should explain your "high" feeling.

Always thinking about that person

When you like someone romantically, it is difficult to get him or her out of your mind. The brain releases a chemical called phenylethylamine, which gives you the feeling of infatuation.

Having the desire to make the person happy

Getting to like someone makes you want to live in their world. Their happiness becomes yours, and so does the sad times. Since happiness is the desired emotion, you will want to go out of your way to make that person happy, even at the expense of your happiness.

The pain is not as intense

Interestingly, once you fall for someone, a literal fall will not feel that pain. A study confirmed that interest and love reduce pain felt, from 40% to about 15%.

Suddenly becoming open to new experiences

Everyone wants to impress someone they like, but if you find yourself wanting to try out the things that the other person likes, you genuinely are smitten.

Gross stuff no longer annoys you

If you are an extreme germaphobe, you are suddenly okay with kissing your partner knowing they haven't brushed their teeth for days. A study confirmed that feelings of love and sexual interest override all the gross feelings.

You sweat more

When you have fallen in love with someone, you tend to show physical symptoms of sickness like excessive sweating, anxiety, stress and a stomach bug. Therefore, the next time you feel unwell, check to see that you are not in love.

The quirks excite you

Chances are you like the things that make the person unique, which possibly what attracted you to them. A study found that quirks cause people to fall in love deeper even than physical appearance does.

11

Identifying Insecurities

I nsecurity means that a person does not feel safe. Insecure people have constantly nagging feeling of not being safe, accepted and okay with whom they are. The biggest issue about insecurity is that it does not come off as plainly as we speak of it because no one wants to admit that he or she lives in constant worry and fear. Therefore, people work very hard to mask or cover up their anxiety with habitual behaviors that most often work against them. The things they do get them the results opposite to what they were seeking.

In case you are unsure of whether someone is insecure, or you feel insecure yourself, below are some of the signs of insecurity that you may recognize:

Signs of Insecurity

He or she talks down how other people look

Someone who does not like how he or she looks will often point at someone else in the room, on social media, or even at the gym. He or she will talk about how the other person looks bad, ugly, has awful clothes, and what the person should have done to look better. This is because the person wants to take off the attention that he assumes that others are giving him from himself to the other person he has pinpointed.

Worries and second-guesses himself in everything

An insecure person will be worried about everything he does. Everything. If he gives a speech, he will be worried that his voice was not loud enough, his laugh was too long or that people did not make notes as he was speaking for which he will wonder whether they got anything from what he said. If the person mops the floor, he will be worried that he did it in a way that did not impress other people. When he wears clothes, he will wonder if he has dressed too light or too heavy for the occasion. While it is normal to ask one person or two what they think about your dressing, the insecure person will want to know what everyone in the room feels. The higher the numbers, the better it is for his confidence.

Keeps pushing you away and pulling you back in

An insecure person will want to pull you in, and as you get closer, the person will suddenly freak out and push you further away. The individual will do this fearing rejection. He will want to drive you away early enough so that you do not get the chance to do it to him. Surprisingly, once you are far away, the person will start begging you to return.

· · ·

The person continually seeks to know whether you are mad and whether what they did has angered you.

Insecurity will have a person constantly asking you whether something he or she did has made you angry. He or she lives in constant worry of losing you, and they figure that if they do not do what you want, how you want it done, you will be gone from their life.

Feels like the entire world hates them

One of the most prominent signs of an insecure person, which comes up in many of the insecure people, is thinking that every other person hates them. If you ask them the reason, the person cannot point to anything in particular that people dislike them for and cannot tell you how they know it. All that the person is sure about is that the people on this earth hate him.

Worries that someone could be speaking ill about him or her

Insecure people are always worried that people are speaking about them behind their backs. They are in constant fear of being scorned, and this insecurity leads them on a search for confirmation that the people around them are not badmouthing them. Usually, there is no reason to even speak about them.

Brags to others

An insecure person longs for others to know about the accomplishments he has made in life or his career. He wants everyone to know the beautiful lady he is dating or that he just bought the latest car model. Do not confuse bragging with confidence or as social media calls it "counting my blessings." This is straight up pride. People who are happy with who they are, what they have done, what is going on in their lives and the miles they have walked have no reason to brag.

Humiliates the people he once knew

A person who is insecure about how he treated or behaved in regard to another person will seek to bad-mouth or defame that other person publicly. Even worse, the person will only offer the side of the story that portrays him as a good person.

People who did not do wrong or play a role that contributed to the fall of the relationship or friendship have no business spoiling another person's reputation. In fact, people with emotional intelligence and integrity are not concerned with the scandals that are raised, they just ignore them, or seek to resolve their issues in private.

Has an excuse for walking down on others

A person that is fully aware that he is wasting other people's time and resources, treating the people as disposables, will always come up with a good reason for doing so. For example, if the person shows up an hour late, does not treat his family and friends with love, or speaks behind another person's back will find a way to justify his behavior. Listening to their excuses, you will notice that they kind of sound noble, but they are not. If you turn around and question this person, he will turn you to be the jerk.

Belittles other people's success

A person who is insecure, driven by the spirit of competition, listens to praises of another person's success, feels that people consider the other person's success superior to what he has achieved and is intimidated by the success starts trying to belittle and demean the superior accomplishments of the other person the best way he can.

However, a person who celebrates other people's success and uses them as inspiration to push himself to achieve greater things is comfortable in who he is, and cannot be considered insecure. He has no need to toughen it out with the guys to prove that he too is powerful.

Wins horribly

An insecure person preemptively strikes at your wins and works hard to cover up the losses he has made in the past. By doing this, the person will be trying to dispel any kind of doubt others around him have in regard to his abilities. A good winner has nothing to prove to other people. They only enjoy their participation in the activity, and when all is done, they disappear back to their private life without bothering others with conceited talk.

Loses Badly

Just as insecure people are poor winners, they are also poor losers. There is nothing an insecure person hates more than losing. People may call it determination, but it is only a ploy to hide their losses. When the person fails, he gives speeches about how manipulative the system is or how the person who won cheated. They will also complain about how the person who won got an unfair advantage and how the insecure person had been watching the exercise for a long time without speaking.

Mocks poor people

A person who is not secure about his level of financial security will sincerely and constantly ridicule those living in poverty and adverse conditions. People who don't define themselves by the amount they make have no business insulting and mocking those whose salaries are low.

Make idle threats

Majority of the time, when an insecure person realizes that his or her insecurities have been found out, or at least that they are under suspicion, he makes threats. If you go ahead and challenge the person's insecurity and the primitive ways of acting out, the person starts threatening you by your job, reputation, and the relationships you have. A person who is secure in who he is will not have a reason to be angry when people know some things about him or her, even the mistakes he has made, because the person believes that those are learning moments.

Does not see the positivity in others

A person who is intimidated by another's achievement, greatness, and good name starts working to bring that other person down. He or she will frantically search for any negative thing you have done and then point it out to other people. His delight will be in ensuring that those that respect you have come to know any negative information and the weaknesses that you have. Surprisingly, the person will stay clear of any strengths and good thing that you have done or said.

Everything said or done is secretly an attack against him

A person who is so insecure and is unable to hide it will think that everything you do or say is a direct jab meant to attack him or her individually. For example, if you have the insecure person for a husband and you stay out late with your girlfriends, once you are back, he will begin asking you whether you stayed out late trying to prove to others that he does not have friends, but you do. In reality, your staying out late had nothing to do with your partner at the very least.

An insecure person will also think that everything that is said around them has ulterior motives and will constantly shuffle the conversation back to himself in an attempt to unravel the motives of everyone that was involved.

Insists on having the last word

Many insecure people like to engage with others in a battle of words as their way of feeling intelligent, authoritative, validated, and to get the sensation that they have been heard. As a result, the person will not concede in a discussion, even when he sees that the other person's argument makes sense, and his no longer does. However, silly his argument is, the person will ensure that he gets the last word, or else he will feel insignificant and inferior.

Wants to bring up your past mistakes and pin them on you

Some people use their mistakes and failures as a way to define themselves that they will not let you get over yours. They look for an opportunity to speak about a mistake you did or a time when your life was not as it is now, and they will make everyone know this. Their job is to have everyone label you by that mistake so that the people will consider the person better than you, or at least, equal to you. A person with this character is not moved by any good thing you did or accomplished; the negatives of your life matter to him or her most.

"Humblebrag"

A humblebrag is a normal brag disguised in a self-derogatory statement. There are too many of these on social media platforms. For example, someone will complain about what a long flight he or she had to endure, but will be grateful that at least, the person was in first-class. Another will complain about how he has to take his kids to expensive places because they demand that of him and he is too weak to say no. Another will complain about how he had to spend the weekend attending his kid's hockey games, but that he is so grateful because they emerged the best players of the season. Too many people on the internet have taken to the humble brag to gloat about their accomplishments.

. . .

Reminds other people about his accomplishments occasionally

You will quickly take note of an insecure person by listening to his or her speech because the person keeps bringing up the things he or she has accomplished. This is an attempt to remind you that under no circumstance should you take him or her lightly. The person will talk about the lifestyle he has managed to get himself, how he has raised intelligent children who are now running large organizations across the world and how long he has sustained a marriage so that you know he is good at relationships. You will also be constantly reminded about how young he was when he made his first million dollars.

Statements like these are the person's way of reminding himself of his worth and making sure that you too will not forget it.

Tries to make you insecure also

The minute you start questioning your self-worth, realize that it is because of the company you have now started keeping. Evaluate the people around your life and see whether any of them keeps broadcasting his achievements to the point that you feel inferior. If you usually do not feel inferior, but you are now starting to, it is likely that the insecure people you have added to your life have begun projecting their insecurities to you.

Complains about how bad things are (or how they are yet to come to a certain level)

People with an inferiority complex will want you to see how high their standards are; you may be tempted to think that they are snobs. However, realize that the person is just putting on an act to charm you and to cause you to see that the person is better than you. It might become tough to shake this feeling. By the high standards they proclaim, insecure people intend to show others that they are better than you are because they hold themselves to higher self-assessment criteria.

The ability to detect the insecurity that people around you project will help you get rid of the self-doubts that being around people like them has implanted in you. If you can avoid engaging with insecure people in your life, do so. Cut the relationship that you have with them. If the people are close to you, take the high road and do not give in to these feelings so that you may cultivate the sense of fulfillment only by what you do, not by comparing your achievements with those of other people.

Conclusion

Thank for making it through to the end of *"Analyze and Influence Anyone – A Psychologist's Guide to Speed-Reading People and Personality Types.* Let's hope it was informative and able to provide you with all of the tools you need to achieve your goals whatever they may be.

Each of us struggles with understanding other people or knowing what their motives are primarily because we are wired differently. However, by getting your hands on comprehensive information that is supported by scientific research, you now have a pretty good idea about how to deal with people and to know what drives them.

One of the most challenging things today is to know another person's true intentions and motives behind what they do or say. A man will approach a woman he has developed a romantic interest in, and she will wonder what his true intentions are. Someone will contact you for business, and you will question whether the person is legit or not. The world is no longer what it used to be, and there is no longer sufficient ground to trust anyone. In our quest to protect ourselves, we have ended up distrusting even primary human emotion.

This book, however, dispels your fears by giving you clues that will guide you towards understanding what could be taking place in a person's most secret thoughts. Once you know how to do it, you will be on your way to dealing with people while reading them and taking caution not to associate with toxic people, or not letting their toxicity get to you. In addition, knowing a person's true intentions will help you avoid being duped, which is now even more common than ever.

The next step is to learn every trick you found applicable to your life by heart and to keep revisiting them so that you can practice this knowledge in your daily endeavors. It will help you be on top of your game so that people do not throw you off of it anyhow.

Finally, if you found this book useful in any way, a review on Amazon is always appreciated!

CPSIA information can be obtained
at www.ICGtesting.com
Printed in the USA
BVHW041051100220
571924BV00008B/132